DISCOVER WATERFORD

EAMONN McENEANEY was educated at De La Salle College, Waterford and Trinity College, Dublin, where he studied history. He was a teacher before being appointed History and Heritage Advisor to Waterford Corporation in 1992. He was involved in the setting up of Waterford Museum of Treasures, Waterford Corporation's flagship tourist attraction, of which he is now manager and curator. He is also curator of Reginald's Tower Museum and managed, on behalf of Waterford Corporation, the restoration of the tower and the installation of the exhibition there. This work was carried out in partnership with Dúchas, The Heritage Service. He is a member of the restoration committee of Christ Church Cathedral, Waterford, and has worked on the installation of an exhibition in the cathedral.

His role in Waterford Corporation has seen him involved with the ongoing restoration of the city's medieval defences, and he was particularly involved with the restoration of the Beach Tower, a joint Waterford Corporation–Waterford Civic Trust project.

He has contributed to various publications, including *Late Viking Age and Medieval Waterford Excavations 1986–1992*, published by Waterford Corporation in 1997, and edited *A History of Waterford and its Mayors*, published in 1995 by Waterford Corporation to celebrate 800 years of civic government in Waterford. He has also written a guide to the city's medieval defences, published by Waterford Corporation, and a guide to Reginald's Tower, published by Dúchas, The Heritage Service.

Discover WATERFORD

EAMONN McENEANEY

THE O'BRIEN PRESS
DUBLIN

For Ann, Conor and Eva

First published 2001 by The O'Brien Press Ltd.,
20 Victoria Road, Dublin 6, Ireland.
Tel: +353 1 4923333; Fax: +353 1 4922777
E-mail books@ obrien.ie
Website www.obrien.ie

ISBN: 0-86278-656-8

British Library Cataloguing-in-Publication Data
A catalogue record for this title is available from the British Library

1 2 3 4 5 6 7 8
01 02 03 04 05 06 07

The O'Brien Press   the**arts**
receives assistance from council
an chomhairle
ealaíon
50⌐

Editing, typesetting, layout and design: The O'Brien Press Ltd.
Modern map of Waterford: Design Image
Colour separations: C&A Print Services Ltd.
Printing: GraphyCEMS

'I heard the mayor say:
"We've had history before now, folks, in this town.
There'll be more history soon".'

Frank Ormsby

ACKNOWLEDGEMENTS

The author would like to thank His Worship the Mayor of Waterford, Alderman Davy Daniels, the Members of Waterford City Council and Eddie Breen, Waterford City Manager and Town Clerk for their support in the writing of this guide. I also acknowledge Dr Eugene Broderick, Jack Burtchaell, Des Cowman, Dan Dowling, Dr Peter Galloway, Mark Girouard, Des Griffin, Martin Hearne, Bill Irish and Julian Walton whose written works or personal comments I relied upon for the compilation of this guide. Orla Scully, the doyenne of Waterford Archaeology, was, as always, a mine of information on the archaeology of Viking Age and medieval Waterford. I am indebted to the following: the very supportive staff at Waterford Museum of Treasures, in particular Rosemary Ryan who was of great assistance with the text and Linda Jacob whose technical expertise was invaluable; the photographers Michelle Brett and Pat McArdle from Waterford Corporation/FÁS, John Power and Terry Murphy for their professionalism and cooperation. A very special thanks to Rachel Pierce of The O'Brien Press for her dedication and resourcefulness, and to Lynn Pierce and Emma Byrne.

Finally to my wife Ann, son Conor and daughter Eva, I owe a great debt of gratitude for their continued support and encouragement.

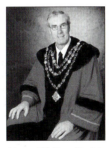

Mayor Ald. Davy Daniels

PICTURE CREDITS

The author and publisher wish to thank the following for permission to reproduce visual materials: Michelle Brett, front cover (bottom), pp.14, 43, 69, 71, 78, 80, 82, 84, 88, 90, 92, 102, 104 (top), 105 (both), 109, colour section: pp.4 (both), 6 (bottom), 7 (bottom), 8 (top), 15 (bottom); Terry Murphy Photography, front cover (middle), pp.17, 20, 22, 24, 25, 26, 28, 29, 32, 33, 34, 60, 67, 68, 73, 75, 98, 99, colour section: pp.7 (top), 9 (both), 10 (bottom), 13 (top); Front cover (top), hand-coloured View of Waterford from Charles Smith's *The Ancient and Present State of the County and City of Waterford* (1746), used by kind permission of Very Rev. Peter Barrett, Dean of Waterford; Map of Ireland, 1339, redrawn by TJ Westropp pl. XLII, RIA, *Proc.*, XXXI, sect. c, 1913, p.21; John Power, p.23, colour section: pp.2 (bottom), 11, 16; Pat McArdle, pp.43, 58, 71, 74, 81, 104 (bottom), colour section, p.8 (bottom); Leo Murphy, photo of Ald. Davy Daniels; The National Gallery of Ireland, p.16; Courtesy of the Board of Trustees of the Victoria and Albert Museum, London, p.47; courtesy of the National Library of Ireland, p.55 (top), 56, 57, 89; Courtesy of The Irish Picture Library, from Fr Browne SJ Collection, p.59; Garter Lane Arts Centre for a photo by Chris Nash, p.94, colour section: p.14 (top); Spraoi, colour section: p.14 (bottom); Courtesy Sir Robert and Lady Goff, p.49 (top); Courtesy of Brendan Grogan, p.107.

CONTENTS

PART ONE: The History of the City

PART TWO: Guide to the Historic City

THE HISTORY OF THE CITY

Discover Waterford

Waterford is the oldest centre of continuous urban settlement in Ireland and is consequently the island's oldest city. It also has the distinction of being older than all of the north European capitals, save London and Paris. Its age is reflected in its name: it is the largest settlement in Ireland to retain its old Norse or Viking-derived place name. Its old Norse name, Vedrarfjord, has two possible meanings. The first is 'windy fjord' or 'haven from the wind-swept sea'. Even today it is easy to see why it may have got this name for the River Suir (pronounced shure) is, even during bad weather, relatively calm and therefore would have been suitable for the sleek Viking longships to drop anchor. The second possible meaning is 'fjord of the rams', that is, a place where rams or sheep could be loaded for export.

Throughout the medieval period and up until the end of the seventeenth century, Waterford remained the second city in Ireland; Dublin was the first city. Today, Waterford is the cultural, economic, educational, technological and industrial capital of the southeast region and its port – the traditional source of its wealth – continues to expand in line with the growth of the Irish economy.

Viking origins

As early as 795, Viking pirates and freebooters had been organising swift and devastating attacks on monasteries and other settlements in Ireland. Their longboats took full advantage of the country's river system, which allowed them to penetrate deep inland and carry off both slaves and treasure with relative ease. By about 850 these Viking raiders found it more convenient to over-winter in Ireland, and so longphorts or ships' havens were established at various locations around the coast. We know from the annals (records written by monks and kept in the monasteries) that a longphort was established at Waterford in 853. The attraction of the Waterford site is

Coins minted in York by Regnall, grandson of Ivor the Boneless. Regnall established the first permanent settlement at Waterford in AD914.

obvious: one-fifth of the land area of Ireland is drained by the Nore, Barrow and Suir, the three rivers that flow into Waterford harbour. For the Vikings, this far-reaching river system was a highway provided by nature and their longships allowed them take full advantage of it. The annals make many references to raiding parties from this base plundering the rich lands around Waterford that were accessible by river.

As with all of the ninth-century Viking bases in Ireland, the base at Waterford appears to have been abandoned by 902, for in that year the annals tell us that 'the foreigners were driven out of Ireland' by the Gaelic Irish. The reappearance of the Vikings in 914 marks the final wave of Viking settlement in Ireland. The Irish annals record that it was at Waterford that they re-established a foothold. In 914 the great Viking adventurer and pirate Regnall, grandson of Ivor the Boneless (apparently his grandfather was impotent), established a base here and built a *longphort*, which would in time become the modern city. In 918, Regnall took a fleet of ships and left Waterford, sailing for York in England. York (Jorvick) was then controlled by Danish Vikings and was perhaps the most important city in the Viking world. After some fierce fighting, Regnall and his fleet captured York and he became the first Norse ruler of that city, dying in 921 as holder of the title: king of Waterford and York. Regnall's dynasty would rule York for fifty years. But Regnall was not simply a brutish raider, he appreciated the importance of trade and as ruler of York he issued coins which were emblazoned on the obverse with the hammer of the Viking god Thor and on the reverse with a bow and arrow.

In the early weeks, months and years of the settlement, security was of paramount importance because Regnall and his war band were intruders in what was for them hostile territory. The site selected for their base had to address the security needs of the new inhabitants as well as the longboats on which their livelihood depended. Accordingly, when the Vikings took up at Waterford they built their *longphort* on a tidal inlet created by the confluence of the Pill (also known as St John's River) and the much larger River Suir. Here the Viking longboats were relatively safe from attack by the Gaelic Irish and from the worst excesses of tide and tempest. Today this tidal inlet is the site of a broad boulevard known as the Mall, created in the eighteenth century when the Pill was diverted so that it entered the River

Suir further downriver and the area it had occupied was reclaimed. Evidence of the original *longphort* was unearthed in 1996 when archaeologists working on the Mall excavated a quay wall and beneath this found a floor timber from a Viking Age ship.

To protect the *longphort* from river-borne attack a fort known as Dundory Fort was built on or close to the site where Reginald's Tower stands today. Dundory Fort became the nucleus of the settlement at Waterford but as those occupying the fort concentrated on piracy the orientation of the settlement was very probably towards the Pill and the tidal inlet.

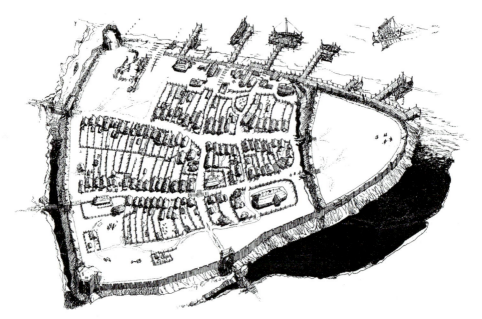

Viking Waterford c.1050. To the north River Suir; dark area represents St John's River.

The site chosen by Regnall for the *longphort* at Waterford was to have a profound impact on the subsequent development and character of the city. Even today, over 1,000 years after the arrival of Regnall, the imprint of the Vikings is still etched on the city's streetscape and Reginald's (ie, Regnall's) Tower, the site of the original settlement, is still a pivotal point in the city's topography. As the settlement gradually developed into a commercial centre and the population expanded, the focus of settlement moved towards the River Suir. This movement away from the Pill, which gave the Viking settlement the distinct street pattern that survives to the present day, had perhaps as much to do with security as with commercial considerations. Foreign trading vessels were probably not permitted to dock in the *longphort* on the Pill as they could pose a security risk, instead it is likely they were encouraged to drop anchor along the banks of the Suir. Local traders and merchants needed to keep a close watch on the trading vessels anchoring at the quays, therefore the focus of commercial activity moved to High Street, which runs parallel to the quays and the Suir. In medieval times this street was known as Booth Street (the street of the shops), and it became the commercial centre of the settlement. Running roughly parallel to High Street were both Peter Street and Lady Lane. The basic triangular shape of the old city had now been formed as these three streets, wedged between the two rivers, converged on Dundory Fort/Reginald's Tower, which stood at the apex of the triangle.

Life in Viking Waterford

Between 1986 and 1992 a fifth of the Viking Age city was excavated, revealing a large portion of Viking Age High Street and Peter Street, and seventy-two houses dating from the eleventh and twelfth centuries. The majority of the houses were single-roomed dwellings with thatched roofs and walls made of wattle sallies woven in a basket-like fashion. In the middle of each house was an open hearth, used for cooking and to provide heat; the smoke escaped through a hole in the roof. In some of the dwellings insulation was provided by a double set of walls with the space between them filled with bracken, dried leaves and moss.

Life for the Viking Age inhabitants of Waterford was short – the average person did not have to worry about mid-life crisis as most were dead by the age of forty. But coping with the in-laws was still a problem for those early settlers as many of the houses uncovered had a 'Granny flat' to the rear! As the houses were made of wattle with a timber mainframe to support the thatch roof fire was a major threat, so at night the fire was covered with a curfew bowl to prevent sparks escaping. Early Waterfordians knew only too well the devastation that could be caused by fire. The town had burnt to the ground on at least four occasions – in 1031, 1037, 1088 and 1111. The first three times were probably the result of warfare. The fire in 1111 was probably caused by a lightning strike as the Irish annals record lightning as the cause of a number of serious fires that year. The fear of fire was so strong in the thirteenth-century town that the city authorities passed a law allowing for the execution of householders, by casting them in the midst of the flames, if they were responsible for an outbreak of fire.

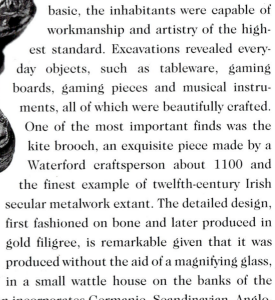

The kite brooch, c.1100, from Waterford city excavations.

Though their homes were relatively basic, the inhabitants were capable of workmanship and artistry of the highest standard. Excavations revealed everyday objects, such as tableware, gaming boards, gaming pieces and musical instruments, all of which were beautifully crafted. One of the most important finds was the kite brooch, an exquisite piece made by a Waterford craftsperson about 1100 and the finest example of twelfth-century Irish secular metalwork extant. The detailed design, first fashioned on bone and later produced in gold filigree, is remarkable given that it was produced without the aid of a magnifying glass, in a small wattle house on the banks of the River Suir. The design incorporates Germanic, Scandinavian, Anglo-Saxon and Gaelic Irish motifs, suggesting that the craftsperson had a very broad repertoire of influences to draw on. The kite brooch is a highly decorated form of the simple dress or stick pin commonly used to fasten cloaks throughout the Viking world. According to Brehon (Gaelic) law, only a lady of high standing could wear a brooch of this quality. The brooch would once have had a very long silver pin that could be cut into pieces and used to trade, just as silver coins were used. If the pin caused an injury to a passer-by then the injured party could, under Brehon law, seek compensation. The kite brooch is unique, but over 250 simple Viking Age pins have been recovered in Waterford, about a quarter of all those found in Europe. These can be seen at Waterford Museum of Treasures.

A number of leather shoes, including children's shoes, were also uncovered during excavations, suggesting that the inhabitants were equipped with more than just the basic necessities. We only have to look at photographs from the 1940s of Waterford children running about barefooted to appreciate just how sophisticated these Viking Age Waterfordians were.

The Viking legacy

From an economic viewpoint, the most enduring legacy of the Vikings was the establishment of Ireland's first commercial centres and ports, which brought Ireland into close contact with Europe. These towns acted as catalysts for change in the religious sphere and also in the body politic. Gaelic princes saw control of the towns as critical to their claim for the high kingship of Ireland, and many employed in battle the fleets maintained by the Viking settlements. In 1137, Diarmait Mac Murchada, king of Leinster, made an unsuccessful attempt to capture Waterford, burning the city in the process. It is interesting to note that when archaeologists discovered part of the earthen bank and ditch that surrounded the Viking city, they also found that it had been upgraded to a stone wall in about 1137 – almost certainly in response to Mac Murchada's attack. This indicates a well-organised municipal system, for the quality of the defences was such that they must have been conceived as a unit and erected by communal effort. Waterford's importance in the Irish political landscape can also be gauged from the fact that the Mc Cartaigh king of Desmond (present-day

Excavated Viking Age defensive ditch and wall, dating to c.1137.

Cork/Kerry region) assisted the Waterfordians when Mac Murchada attacked, and had also come to their aid during an earlier siege in 1088.

The conversion of the Vikings

While the town's merchants imported iron, luxury cloths, pottery and, of course, fine wine, the basic food requirements were supplied by the farmsteads that existed on the edge of the city. The names of some of these early farmsteads survive in the names of modern suburbs, such as Ballytruckle or the homestead of Torcal, derived from the Viking chieftain Torcal or Turgesius, and Ballygunner or the homestead of Gunnar. These outlying farms were in turn surrounded by the Christian Gaelic Irish. Political alliances and intermarriage with their Gaelic neighbours meant that in time the Vikings were converted to Christianity.

Interior of Christ Church Cathedral.

In 1096 Malchus, the first bishop of Waterford, was consecrated in England by Anselm, archbishop of Canterbury. It was the O'Brien kings of Munster who had made the request to Canterbury for a bishop to minister to the people of Waterford, seeing this intervention as a means of increasing their status. Bishoprics and dioceses were new to Ireland, where from the earliest times the monasteries had played a leading role in Church organisation. The establishment of the first Irish dioceses, Dublin, followed by Waterford in 1096, was one of the early steps in bringing the Irish Church in line with that on the continent. It is ironic that the descendants of the Vikings, whose forebears have gone down in Irish history as pagans who plundered the monasteries, should be in the vanguard of Church reform in the late eleventh century.

Waterford's first cathedral was located on the site of the present Church of Ireland cathedral. There have been several buildings on this site, and a recently discovered chevron-decorated stone, part of an arch, is all that remains above ground of the Romanesque cathedral where, on 25 August 1170, following the fall of the Viking Age city to the Anglo-Normans, the most famous marriage in Irish history took place.

The coming of the Anglo-Normans

Following his violent struggle for the high kingship, the great enemy of Waterford, Diarmait Mac Murchada, was expelled from Ireland in 1066 and fled to Bristol in England. Diarmait was fêted by that city's rich merchant class, many of whom had economic ties with him through trading with the merchants of Dublin, a city he controlled until 1166. From Bristol, Diarmait went in search of King Henry II of

England, carrying with him the hope of obtaining the king's permission to recruit mercenaries in England and Wales to help him recover his lost kingdom. He finally caught up with Henry in France and was well received by the king who, in 1165, had hired the Dublin fleet from Diarmait for six months while campaigning in Wales. Having offered fealty to Henry, Diarmait received permission to recruit mercenaries. It was the widowed Richard de Clare (Strongbow), earl of Pembroke, who answered Diarmait's plea for help. However, Strongbow was no mercenary: he would fight only for land. Diarmait therefore promised to give him the hand of his own daughter, Aoife, in marriage and thereby make him heir to the kingdom of Leinster should he agree to cross to Ireland with an army and reinstate him, Diarmait, as king of Leinster.

Anglo-Norman intervention in Ireland begun in earnest when Robert Fitz Stephen landed at Bannow Bay in County Wexford in 1169. In May 1170, Raymond le Gros arrived with a small army at Baginbun in County Wexford. On that occasion the men of Waterford, sensing that the Normans were too close for comfort, decided to dislodge them with the aid of their Gaelic allies from the Decies (County Waterford). Using an old Iron Age fortification as a base, the small Anglo-Norman army rounded up a large number of cattle, which they brought inside the earthen defences. When the men of Waterford arrived the cattle were driven out against them, causing havoc in the lines of the advancing army. The Waterfordians and their allies were defeated and seventy men were taken as prisoners. Gerald of Wales, the Anglo-Norman chronicler, tells us that the prisoners were handed over to Alice of Abervenny, a Welsh woman, who, wielding an axe of tempered steel, beheaded them to a man. It appears that earlier that day her lover, a Norman mercenary, had lost his life in battle and this was her bloody revenge.

But worse was to come for Waterford, thanks to the scheming of Mac Murchada. On 23 August, Strongbow besieged the city and it fell to him on 25 August. The stone walls the citizens had built in 1137 were no match for the Anglo-Normans. Gerald of Wales informs us that the Anglo-Normans noticed a small wooden building overhanging the town wall and supported by props outside the wall. They removed the props and the building came crashing down, bringing with it part of the defensive wall. Through this breach they entered, slaughtering the inhabitants and burning their homes. The citizens were overwhelmed; Strongbow then sent for Mac Murchada and Aoife, and in Christ Church Cathedral, amid the ruins, the most important marriage in Irish history took place. The marriage of Strongbow and Aoife in Waterford marked the end of the Viking Age in Irish history and the beginning of English involvement in Irish affairs.

The Marriage of Princess Aoife of Leinster with Richard de Clare, Earl of Pembroke (Strongbow). By Daniel Maclise (1806–1870).

The arrival of Henry II

Henry II was alarmed by Strongbow's success, fearing that he might attempt to establish a rival kingdom in Ireland. The king therefore decided to put his mark on a process of colonisation that was taking place almost despite him. Henry II arrived in Waterford in 1171 – the first time an English king had set foot in an Irish city. He took submissions from both Gaelic princes and Anglo-Norman lords, and removed from Strongbow's control the port cities of Waterford and Dublin. Waterford now became a royal city.

Anglo-Norman success in Ireland was due in part to the fact that there was no central authority capable of resisting invasion, and also because the Church, one of the most powerful institutions in Ireland, saw Henry II as a reformer. The king could, under the terms of the bull *Laudabiliter* (proclaimed sixteen years earlier), claim to have papal backing for the invasion and the reform of the Church in Ireland. His aim was to bring the Church into line with practice on the continent.

Strongbow's involvement in Irish affairs, though not part of Henry II's master plan, could be turned to the advantage of the king who was now in the pope's bad books. The struggle between Church and State that had occupied much of Henry's reign had taken a turn for the worse in 1170 when his agents assassinated that great upholder of papal authority, Thomas à Beckett, archbishop of Canterbury. Now Henry could curb the ambitions of the Anglo-Norman lords in Ireland and at the same time placate the pope by instigating the reform of the Irish Church. In turn, Henry's backing for the reform of the Church helped to legitimise his position in Ireland. Within days of Henry's arrival some members of the Irish hierarchy met in the cathedral at Waterford and pledged their support for the reform of the Church. Remarkably, *Laudabiliter,* once thought to be the main reason for Henry's arrival, was not publicly read in Ireland until 1173, at a synod of bishops in Christ Church Cathedral, Waterford.

King John and the medieval city

In 1177 Henry II appointed John, his youngest son, as lord of Ireland. (John, Henry's favourite, was nicknamed Lackland because until he was appointed lord of Ireland, his father had no land to give him.) John was spoilt by his father and in 1185, in compensation for his refusal to let John go to the Holy Land on crusade, Henry sent him to Ireland. John landed at Waterford in May and immediately raised the hackles of the Gaelic princes who had come to meet him by 'pulling at their long beards'. The prince ordered the re-fortification of the old Viking city; the construction of the ground and first floors of the present Reginald's Tower were begun at this time. John is also known to have endowed the city's Benedictine priory, the ruins of which are close to the city walls at Manor Street. Both the priory and the river that runs

King John, 1199–1216, from the Great Charter Roll, Waterford.

close to it are dedicated to St John, a dedication undoubtedly influenced by the prince.

An almost contemporary Anglo-Norman account of John's visit, written by Gerald of Wales, claims that John confined himself to the towns and that both he and his young friends gave themselves to wine and women. John partook of so much wine, cider and fresh Irish salmon that he became ill, and fearing that he had contracted leprosy promised the Almighty that he would build a leper hospital if spared. He survived and a leper hospital was built in Waterford, dedicated to St Stephen. All that remains of the hospital today is the house of the hospital master, rebuilt in 1637.

When John revisited the city in 1210 he came not only as lord of Ireland but also as king of England, for fate had conspired to ensure the maintenance of political links between Ireland and England. In 1199, with the death of Richard I, all of Henry's sons were dead and without legitimate heirs, thus his hope of creating a separate kingdom in Ireland for John came to nothing. So upon Richard I's death in 1199, John became ruler of the two countries.

It was almost certainly during his second visit to Waterford in 1210 that John endowed the cathedral with lands, and it was about this time also that the Gothic-style Christ Church Cathedral was built. On an economic level, John encouraged trade by granting the city the right to hold an annual fair, which helped to attract foreign merchants to Waterford. He also encouraged both foreign and domestic trade by establishing a mint in the city. Silver coins were struck in Waterford when John was lord of Ireland, and again when he was both lord of Ireland and king of England. In 1215, within weeks of being forced to issue *Magna Carta* to the barons at Runnymead, the king granted Waterford a charter, the terms of which imply that by the end of his reign a sophisticated system of local government had evolved, which saw elected representatives of the merchant class controlling almost all of the internal affairs of the city.

Early thirteenth-century pottery money box, a coin balance, coins and a tally stick.

During John's reign the merchants who settled in the city in the wake of the Anglo-Norman invasion were both

prosperous and sophisticated. They controlled the export of the huge agricultural
surplus that was now coming on stream
thanks to the agricultural improvements
introduced both by the Anglo-Norman
landholders and by the new religious
houses established by them. While agricultural produce was exported in large
quantities, imports were mainly luxuries,
such as wine and fine cloth, along with

Coin balance, c.1200, used to determine
the weight of a silver coin.

more practical commodities, such as salt and iron. At this time also
we find ships bringing Dundry stone to Waterford from quarries near
Bristol in England. The stone was popular because it is easy to carve;
much of the stone used in the Gothic Christ Church
Cathedral came from Dundry. In an age when
exports were booming and imports low, it is safe
to presume that the stone was also used by
mariners as ballast.

The wealth and sophistication of individual
merchants may be appreciated from their
personal objects and household goods, many
of which were found during excavations. Perhaps the finest find is the famous ring brooch, on
display at Waterford Museum of Treasures.
Made from twenty-two carat gold, the ring
brooch is the oldest of its type in Europe and
was probably made in Waterford around
1210. It was made as a love-token, commis-

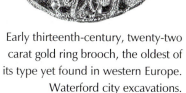

Early thirteenth-century, twenty-two
carat gold ring brooch, the oldest of
its type yet found in western Europe.
Waterford city excavations.

sioned by a wealthy merchant or a knight for presentation to a lady of
some social standing.

Control of the harbour

John died in 1216 and was succeeded by his son, Henry III. However,
Henry was only nine years old so his father decreed that William Marshall, one of the wealthiest men in England, would rule until Henry
came of age. William Marshall had married Strongbow and Aoife's
daughter, Isobel, and by this marriage the old Mac Murchada lands of
Leinster were added to his vast estates in both England and France.

Marshall, a very enterprising man, envied the profits being made by the royal ports of Dublin and Waterford from agricultural exports that were produced on his lands in Leinster. To exploit the rich seam of exports he decided to build a new port, New Ross, through which the produce of Leinster could be exported to his benefit. New Ross, located on the River Barrow, which enters the sea at Waterford Harbour, was to become a serious rival to the port of Waterford. Sharing the same harbour, Waterford and New Ross now vied with each other for the lion's share

King Henry III, 1216–1272, from the Great Charter Roll, Waterford.

of the import and export trade. Marshall encouraged trade by building Hook Lighthouse around 1200 – the oldest operational lighthouse in Europe today.

While William Marshall was ruler of England, he tried to give every advantage possible to New Ross. However, when Henry III took control of the government in 1219 following the death of Marshall, Waterford pressed its case and succeeded in getting the new king to reaffirm the claimed rights of Waterford, that is, that all foreign ships entering Waterford Harbour must unload at Waterford, and that only ships from the lordship of Leinster (Diarmait Mac Murchada's old kingdom) could call at New Ross.

Reginald's Tower.

Waterford: the wine capital of Ireland

Henry III never visited Ireland, but he did give the citizens of Waterford the right to levy taxes to finance the enclosing of a large extension to the city, which was required to cater for the ever-increasing population. By the end of Henry III's reign in 1272 the suburbs had been enclosed with what was probably a mixture of structures, including stone-built walls and towers. Between 1224 and 1246 three murage grants were granted to fund the building of the walls, allowing the authorities to collect a tax on incoming goods. According to the terms of the grant of 1243, there was a tax of one penny on every 100 salmon, conger and mullet that came through the gates. For 100 skins of lamb, kid and squirrel you paid a half-penny, and for 100 pounds of wax or pepper the tax was two pence.

In 1226 Henry III granted the city authorities permission to give to the Dominicans a piece of ground within the old city in what is today called Conduit Lane. Geoffrey of Waterford, a monk who lived here in the thirteenth century, was highly regarded as a wine expert. It is appropriate that thirteenth-century Waterford should have its own wine expert for during the medieval period the city was the wine capital of Ireland, as recognised in a charter given to the city by Henry III in 1232. This allowed

Thirteenth-century French wine jugs. Waterford city excavations.

the city authorities to pay only half the usual tax on imported wine to ensure that the royal port flourished. The tax on wine imports was called the prise of wine and comprised one barrel of wine from before the ship's mast and one from behind. The tax returns of Henry's reign show that Waterford imported far more wine that any other Irish port. When Gerald of Wales came to Ireland in the 1180s, he wrote that wine was so plentiful you would scarcely believe that the vine was not cultivated here. Its popularity is understandable when we consider that people in the Middle Ages never drank water, considering it a danger to their health, and, of course, tea and coffee had not yet been introduced into Europe.

During the thirteenth century wine came mainly from the Bordeaux region in France, at that time part of the territory of the Anglo-Norman kings of England. The wine ships brought with them pottery wine jugs produced in the Saintonge region just north of Bordeaux. The remains of hundreds of

Map of Ireland, 1339.

these jugs were recovered during excavations in Waterford, and some beautiful examples, which would have adorned the tables of the wine taverns and homes of thirteenth-century Waterford, are now on display at Waterford Museum of Treasures.

Despite the economic prosperity arising from its location, not everyone living in medieval Waterford was a wealthy merchant. The poor of the city, and there were many, had no social welfare, so when they fell on hard times they relied on the charity of the Franciscans. The substantial ruins of the order's thirteenth-century friary and its fifteenth-century bell tower are open to the public, situated in Greyfriars Street.

An age of prosperity

King Edward I, 1272–1307, from the Great Charter Roll, Waterford.

When Henry died in 1272, Waterford was, after Dublin, the largest and wealthiest city in Ireland. Well defended, it boasted many fine buildings, including some ten churches within the walls. Edward I, known as The Hammer of the Scots and as Edward Longshanks, succeeded Henry III and was crowned king in 1274. It was Edward who, as lord of Ireland (a position conferred on him by his father in 1254), gave the citizens the right to elect a mayor. This right can be viewed as the final stage in the development of municipal government, a process that had been ongoing since at least 1195. Today in the foyer of city hall is a list of over 600 named mayors of Waterford. The earliest named mayor is Roger le Lom in 1284; each year the outgoing mayor affixes his name to the list.

Edward was involved in many wars, particularly in Wales and Scotland, and he used the ports of Ireland and England to collect provisions and ship them to his troops. Edward was also the first English monarch to engage in winter campaigns and the financial pressure this placed on his resources forced him to introduce a new tax, called the Great New Custom, levied on exports of wool and hides from England and Ireland. However, because Edward had raised loans from Italian merchant bankers, he was now forced to assign the proceeds of the Great New Custom to them. The Italians demanded the right to collect these taxes personally at the Irish and English ports.

The agents sent to do so came from Lombardy and were known collectively as Lombards. In time, Lombard became a family name and their descendants still live in Waterford today. Lombards are listed as mayors of the city in the fourteenth, fifteenth, sixteenth and seventeenth centuries. One of seventeenth-century Ireland's most famous clergymen, Peter Lombard, archbishop of Armagh and confidant of the pope, was another Waterford-born descendant.

Thirteenth-century seal matrix with bird motif and inscribed with the name Gavin Comerford, probably belonging to a weaver or other artisan. Waterford city excavations.

Edward's reign marked a period of unprecedented growth and prosperity for Waterford as foreign merchants flocked to the city, bringing with them their knowledge of markets, and many made Waterford their home. In 1307 Eymar de Godar, a wine merchant from Gascony in France, was elected mayor – just one of a number of foreigners who held the post during Edward's reign. Edward also established a mint in Waterford under the control of Stephen Fulbourne, bishop of Waterford and governor of Ireland.

However, while Edward's reign marked the high point in the development of the medieval city, it also marked a turning-point in the success and stability of the Anglo-Norman colony in Ireland. During his reign the Gaelic kings and princes began to reassert themselves and yet, despite the relative prosperity of the colony, the central government in Dublin was unable to properly finance wars against them because the funds had been diverted for Edward's wars abroad. When Edward died in 1307 he had subdued the Scots, but at a price in Ireland of leaving the Anglo-Norman colony vulnerable.

Early thirteenth-century metal belt-mount depicting St Margaret holding the head of a slain dragon, which was, according to legend, presented to her by St George. A symbol of chivalry, the belt from which it came was possibly presented by a lady of social standing to a knight. Waterford city excavations.

Edward I was succeeded by his son, Edward II, whose reign was plagued by court intrigue and civil war. Robert Bruce, king of Scotland, won major victories against the English and his brother, Edward Bruce, invaded Ireland and won the support of many of the Gaelic princes and quite a few Anglo-Norman lords. Though the Bruce invasion failed to reinstate the Gaelic princes, it was nonetheless a major boost and they continued to make gains at the expense of the Anglo-Normans. The problems of the colony were compounded when the Anglo-Normans married into and allied with ruling Gaelic families. Gradually, during the fourteenth century, the descendants of the Anglo-Normans became more Irish than the Irish themselves.

War and plague: the end of an era

A port city like Waterford, dependant on exchanging the produce of the countryside for imported luxuries that were then sold to the inhabitants of the countryside, tried not to become embroiled in the complex series of alliances and feuds that often involved a mixture of both Gaelic Irish and Anglo-Norman

Thirteenth-century pilgrim badges. The circular badge depicts the head of St John the Baptist, that is, the relic of the saint's head as taken from Constantinople following its fall to crusaders in 1204 and brought to Amiens in France, which then became a popular centre for pilgrimage. The square badge depicts the martyrdom of a now unidentifiable saint.

interests. The Bruce invasion of 1315 had highlighted the vulnerability of the Dublin administration. Lack of finance led to a change of emphasis in the government of the lordship as central government began to rely more and more on the local magnates to keep the peace. In theory this was a good idea because the magnates were powerful and it was in their best interests to maintain law and order. However, rivalry between the Anglo-Norman families, their gradual gaelicisation and their military and marriage alliances with the Gaelic Irish all combined to ensure that they could not be relied upon. Peace existed when it suited the local lords and wars were fought not to protect the king's territory but because they promoted local political ambitions.

In east County Waterford the Power family, based at Dunhill, was the principal Anglo-Norman authority. During the fourteenth century the family became involved in all manner of disputes and alliances, which were to have disastrous consequences for Waterford city. By the late 1320s the Munster area, which had escaped the worst effects of the Bruce invasion, was plunged into political and economic turmoil. Capturing the sentiments of the time, an anonymous poet penned the following lines around 1330:

> Young men of Waterford learn how to fight,
> For your ploughshares are being carried off.
> Burnish your weapons that have long been unused,
> And defend yourself against the Powers who are
> patrolling the roads.

Dunhill Castle, home of the Anglo-Norman Power family, barons of Dunhill.

The accession of King Edward III to the throne in England in 1327 did little to improve the situation for Waterford, as the central government in Dublin were almost powerless to prevent the outbreak of private wars. In 1345 the Powers, based in County Waterford, destroyed the countryside around the city.

Four years later a more deadly enemy descended in the form of a plague known as the Black Death, and at least one-third of the city perished. The resultant sharp decline in population across Europe saw a corresponding fall in the demand for goods, particularly catastrophic for a port city like Waterford. However, the merchant class went out and sought fresh opportunities, establishing branches of their export business in English ports where it was easier to find markets. By the end of the fourteenth century so many merchants of Anglo-Irish stock had set up in Bristol that the city council there made moves to prevent them from becoming members of the city council.

In 1368 Waterford was once again subject to attack by the Powers, this time allied to a Gaelic family, the O'Driscolls, from Baltimore in County Cork. John Malpas, a merchant with extensive trading

King Edward III, 1327–1377, from the Great Charter Roll, Waterford.

interests in Bristol, was mayor at the time. This situation called for more than business acumen; Malpas's army was defeated and the records tell that he was 'all hewn and cut to pieces and his body was brought back into the city and immediately buried in the Cathedral'. Six weeks later the Powers and the O'Driscolls were back again, this time getting to the very gates of the city, and a major battle took place on St John's Bridge, just outside St John's Gate, but on this occasion the mayor was victorious.

To add to the city's woes there was also a concerted effort on behalf of New Ross to persuade the king to terminate Waterford's monopoly on ships entering the harbour. The lord of New Ross was a close friend of King Edward III, and it looked certain that the king would grant equal trading rights to both ports. However, faint heart never won fair lady, and in 1372 the mayor searched the city archives for documents to prove that Waterford had received a trading monopoly from Edward III's predecessors. The city's charters and other documents were stitched together to form a long roll measuring some four metres in length. To flatter the king, beautiful coloured illustrations of the monarch and five of his ancestors, together with some ten governors and the mayors of Dublin, Waterford, Cork and Limerick, were attached to the roll. It appears to have won over the king as he allowed the city retain its trading privileges over New Ross. In a letter sent to Edward III in 1373, the mayor outlined the importance of the city to the king when he wrote:

> Waterford, no more than seven acres of land within its walls, is like a little castle, and if all the land of Ireland were gained by the king's enemies it could be better regained by means of our city.

The point was well made, and while King Edward never came to Waterford, he did understand its strategic importance.

Edward's successor, Richard II, decided that something had to be done about Ireland and, in particular, about the Mc Murrough Kavanaghs of the Wicklow Mountains who were organising raiding parties as far north as Dublin and south to Wexford. So in 1394 he embarked on an expedition to Ireland, the first English monarch to

King Richard II landing at Waterford, from Froissart's *Chronicle*.

do so since John in 1210. Richard's arrival up the River Suir at the head of over 500 ships, the largest fleet ever to sail into an Irish port, must have been a magnificent sight. Not so magnificent was the disembarking, as Froissart, Richard's chronicler, tells us 'they waded up to their waist in ooze' while getting from the ships to dry land. (Thankfully, today's river-borne visitors are spared this indignity for outside Reginald's Tower where the king awkwardly disembarked is a modern marina.) At Greyfriars, where he had probably taken up lodgings, Richard accepted the submission of Turloch O'Connor Don of Connaught. During his stay he also attended the installation of the first bishop of the newly united dioceses of Waterford and Lismore. The new bishop, Robert Reed, is said to have intoned the *Te Deum* as the king entered Christ Church Cathedral for his first Mass in Waterford. Richard failed to control the Irish of the Wicklow Mountains however, as they knew that the Dublin government did not have the resources to curb their activities.

Richard returned to Ireland in 1399, again landing at Waterford. However, within weeks of his arrival he received news of the return of the exiled Henry Bolingbroke, earl of Hereford. Alarmed, Richard returned home in haste, but was captured and deposed; Bolingbroke became King Henry IV of England. Throughout the fifteenth century all attempts to restore royal authority in Ireland to the level enjoyed in the thirteenth century failed, and to a great extent cities like Waterford were left to their own devices. The city was often forced to wage war against its enemies and to make payments of protection money or black rents to prevent piracy of its ships and supplies. The enemies of the city included both the Gaelic Irish and the ever-persistent Powers.

The Gaelic O'Driscoll family from Cork, previously allies of the Anglo-Norman Powers, had a particular liking for the Spanish and

Portuguese wine being shipped up the Bay of Biscay and along the south Irish coast to Waterford. During the Hundred Years' War the English monarchy had lost the wine-producing areas of western France, and that in turn led to the development of the Spanish and Portuguese wine trade with its more perilous sea journey. Black rents were being paid to the O'Driscolls by Waterford merchants to secure safe passage for the wine ships and the fishing fleets that were exploiting the rich herring shoals off the Cork coast. However, on Christmas Eve 1413, the mayor of Waterford, Simon Wicken, sailed to Baltimore to teach the O'Driscolls a lesson. Wicken gained admittance to their home under the pretence of paying his black rent: a cargo of wine. Once he had lulled the O'Driscolls into a false sense of security, he captured The O'Driscoll (the head of the clan) and his six sons and then proceeded to hold a carol service! The O'Driscolls were

Mayor of Waterford (top right), c.1372, from the Great Charter Roll, Waterford.

taken as hostages to Waterford 'to sing their carols and make merry that Christmas'. Reaching the city on the night of the Feast of St Stephen (26 December), they found the city walls lit with torches to welcome home the heroic mayor. As for the O'Driscolls, no doubt their family paid a ransom and, much chastised, they returned home to live to fight another day.

The mayor's action against the O'Driscolls was, strictly speaking, illegal for it was the prerogative of the government in Dublin to make war and negotiate peace. However, the reality of the situation in which the city found itself was recognised in 1447 when parliament empowered the mayor to make war: 'he could ride with banners displayed against the Powers, Daltons, Walshes and Grants [all families of Anglo-Norman origin] who were for a long time traitors and rebels and who were constantly robbing the king's subjects of Waterford.'

Late medieval revival

The last major fifteenth-century conflict with the O'Driscolls and the Powers took place in 1461 when The O'Driscoll arrived at Tramore, County Waterford. The mayor prepared a small army and in the ensuing fight several of the O'Driscolls and ten of the Powers were slain. Among the prisoners taken for ransom was The O'Driscoll Óg, together with six of his sons and three of their galleys. Some believe that the three galleys emblazoned on the coat of arms of Waterford represent these captured O'Driscoll galleys.

In many ways the defeat of the O'Driscolls was a pyrrhic victory. In the mayoral election that followed shortly after the victory no one was willing to accept the office. The new king of England, Edward IV, was made aware of the crisis in the city, however his position was precarious and there was little he could do to prevent attacks like this. So instead he bought time and tried to ensure that Waterford remained a loyal outpost by cancelling the city's debts, giving the citizens a new charter and the mayor a gift of a bearing sword, 'to be carried before the Mayor on ceremonial occasions just as the mayor of Bristol does'.

Yet despite the crisis in its government the city still remained an important force on the island. The 1463 parliament met in Waterford where it passed an act establishing a mint in Reginald's Tower. This was a great boost to trade, and late fifteenth-century Waterford, despite some political upheaval, was, like the rest of Europe, experiencing something of an economic boom. There was a major wall-building programme and during the 1460s the dean of the cathedral, John

Bearing swords. The smaller sword was presented to the mayor by King Edward IV in 1462, while the larger one was a gift of King Henry VIII in 1536.

Collyn, even founded an almshouse for the aged poor of the city called the Good Mens' House, located close to the cathedral. The hostel was supported by rents received from land and properties, which were donated by the leading citizens to Collyn for that purpose. Chief among the benefactors was one James Rice, who gave the institution the following: '6 houses and gardens, 3 shops, 2 and a quarter gardens, rents to the value of 30 shillings and other tenements of unspecified value.'

Two of the buildings donated by James Rice to Collyn's almshouse have been located. In High Street the wall of one of these buildings remains and forms part of the Wine Vault restaurant and wine store, which is very appropriate as Rice was almost certainly a wine merchant. The second building was given by Rice to Collyn on 26 July 1468 and has been identified as the north deanery undercroft.

James Rice: merchant prince

James Rice dominated late fifteenth-century Waterford and his life provides us with a window through which we can see, in some detail, the workings of a late medieval Irish city, an historical luxury that is unique to Waterford. Evidence of this remarkable man still remains in Christ Church Cathedral, where Rice's macabre cadaver tomb still rests, and in City Hall, where he has the honour of appearing eleven times in the mayoral list, a distinction unequalled by any other mayor.

James, son of Peter Rice, mayor of Waterford in 1426, was first elected mayor in 1467. A religious man, he accepted the position on eleven occasions out of a deep sense of duty; during this period there was little enthusiasm for the office. As mayor he enacted legislation that was intended both to spread the burden of office and to cajole or encourage other councillors to accept the position if elected, but this met with little success. Despite his best efforts, Rice was not relieved of the task.

In 1482 he accepted the office on condition that he could appoint a deputy because he was planning a pilgrimage to Santiago de Compostella in Spain in 1483. The tomb of the apostle St James at Compostella was, after Jerusalem and Rome, regarded as one of the holiest shrines in Christendom. That year, 1483, was the jubilee year of St James and the pope would give a special indulgence to pilgrims. Such pilgrimages were not for the faint-hearted. The Irish annals and the Anglo-Irish chronicles record the deaths of many important Irish pilgrims either while on pilgrimage or immediately after their return. The gruelling sea journey and the inhospitable conditions, coupled with the threat of robbery or assault by brigands or, worse, pirates on the open seas were all well-known hazards.

James was required to receive permission of both the Irish parliament and King Richard III of England to travel to Spain. On 28 March

1482, with his travel plans in hand, Rice went about the serious business of preparing a tomb for himself should things go wrong. His cadaver tomb is regarded as the finest in Ireland, and it can be seen in the eighteenth-century Christ Church Cathedral, although the chapel

Tomb of James Rice, 1482, Christ Church Cathedral.

in which it was housed was demolished along with the Gothic cathedral in 1773. The top of Rice's *mensa* or table tomb has a representation of a partially decomposed corpse with vacant eye sockets and toads and worms crawling through the cadaver. The inscription reads:

> Here lies James Rice, one time citizen of this city,
> founder of this chapel, and Catherine Brown his wife.
> Whoever you may be passer by,
> Stop, weep as you read,
> I am what you are going to be,
> And I was what you are.
> I beg of you pray for me.

The tomb was housed in a side chapel dedicated to SS Catherine and James and was completed in just nine months. It was consecrated by the bishop of Ossory on 6 December 1482, in time for Rice's departure to Compostella in 1483.

Northwest prospect of Christ Church Cathedral, from James Ware's *Bishops of Ireland* (ed. Walter Harris, 1739). The small chapel furthest from the belfry was known as Rice's Chapel and it contained his tomb.

Rice deliberately invited the bishop of Ossory and not the bishop of Waterford and Lismore, Nicholas O'Hennessy, to consecrate the chapel. He did so because he and John Collyn, dean of the cathedral, had refused to admit or accept the Irish-speaking O'Hennessy, who had been appointed bishop of Waterford and Lismore in 1480. Rice claimed that O'Hennessy was an unsuitable candidate as he did not speak English. Pope Sextus IV was furious and in December 1482 he wrote that dean John Collyn, and especially James Rice, a layman and citizen of the city, had alleged that the previous bishop had not resigned, therefore they refused to receive O'Hennessy as bishop. In fact, the former bishop of Waterford had resigned, but Rice and Collyn, through their influence with Richard III, persuaded him to retract his resignation. Only when a suitable English-speaking candidate was found was the former bishop allowed to formally resign.

Latin inscription from the Great Parchment Book, 1361–1649.

The instance of O'Hennessy's appointment and his alleged unsuitability brought to a head the attitude of the ruling class in the city to the Gaelic Irish. In this period several laws were passed that attempted to curb the use of Gaelic fashion, habits and speech. The legislation clearly shows that customs and traditions of this most Anglo-Norman city were being swamped by the traditions and customs of their Gaelic neighbours. Rice was fighting a rearguard action to preserve English customs in Waterford. What had helped to maintain these customs so long was the constant contact with England through trade, and the presence of colonies of English merchants in the city during the fourteenth and fifteenth centuries. It is interesting that Waterford's Great Parchment Book, which records ordinances of the city council from 1361 to 1649, represents the earliest use, for official purposes, of the English language in Ireland. There is much evidence to suggest that the book in its present form (on display in Waterford Museum of Treasures) was compiled in the 1480s under the direction of James Rice.

Seal of James Rice, medieval Waterford's most famous mayor.

Rice was bailiff (deputy mayor) and James Butler was mayor when the earl of Kildare (the king's lord deputy in Ireland) threatened to hang the city council at their doorposts if they did not accept the pretender to the English throne, Lambert Simnel. The earl of Kildare had crowned Simnel king of England in Christ Church Cathedral in Dublin. However, the city council refused to either accept Simnel or to have him proclaimed king in the city. When the commotion died down and the pretender was deposed, Henry VII sent Richard Edgecombe to receive the submissions of the rebel Irish and Anglo-Irish lords.

When Edgecombe visited Waterford, the mayor gave him lodgings in his home and brought him on a tour of the city to view the defensive walls and towers. Rice's last great public act took place the night Edgecombe was being entertained in the Guild Hall, when he recited the famous poem 'The Mayor of Waterford's Letter', a ballad royal of over 300 lines reviling the archbishop and people of Dublin for their treachery in supporting Simnel. Edgecombe was thus made aware of both Waterford's loyalty and the fact that the earl of Kildare, the king's deputy, disliked the city. Edgecombe promised that Waterford would no longer be harassed by the earl of Kildare or by the Dublin government, and that the city was in fact outside their control. So by the end of the fifteenth century, Waterford had become an all but independent city, giving allegiance to a distant and, for the present at least, relatively weak monarch. In recognition of the city's loyalty, Henry VII sent the city a new charter and the money to purchase 200 bows, 400 bow strings and 9,600 arrows.

James Rice is thought to have died in 1488 and was buried with great pomp and ceremony in the tomb he had prepared.

Urbs Intacta: the untaken city

In 1495 the supporters of yet another pretender, Perkin Warbeck, laid siege to the city. With cannon mounted on the rails of their ships they began the first artillery siege of an Irish city. Waterford was relatively well prepared with guns installed along the wall and on the towers. After an eleven-day assault and the sinking of some of Warbeck's ships, the siege was lifted. One hundred years ago a dredger lifted from the river-bed a small cannon gun that almost

The oldest cannon in Ireland, from the siege of Waterford by Perkin Warbeck in 1495.

certainly came from one of Warbeck's sunken ships. The gun is identical to those borne on the *Nina* when Columbus discovered America in 1492, and it is the oldest cannon gun in Ireland (now on display in Waterford Museum of Treasures).

As a reward for routing Warbeck, King Henry VII gave the city the motto *Urbs Intacta Manet Waterfordia* (Waterford remains the untaken city), to this day emblazoned on the city's arms. Waterford was now a most favoured city; its merchant class held high government office. William Wyse, whose grandfather was mayor and whose father was one of the principal Irish judges, was even brought up at the royal court and became a member of Henry VIII's household, holding the position of Dapifer of the Chamber, responsible for serving meals to the royal family. A few years later he was made Officer of the Wardrobe, which involved keeping the household accounts. In 1520 he was one of eight pages who accompanied King Henry VIII at the king's famous meeting with the king of France at the Field of Cloth of Gold, near Calais in France. Wyse was well rewarded by the king, and in 1515 was appointed constable of Dublin Castle. Through the influence of Cardinal Wolsey he then secured the post of Receiver of the Customs at Bristol. In 1523 he was made constable of Limerick Castle. Wyse's native city was also viewed favourably by the king and he granted the city three new charters.

Wyse returned to Waterford in the 1520s and was elected mayor in 1534. In that year Silken Thomas rebelled against the king, believing rumours that his father, Gearóid Óg FitzGerald, earl of Kildare and lord deputy of Ireland, had been executed in the tower of London. Waterford, under William Wyse, provided a secure base at which troops and supplies could be landed to crush the rebellion. The defeat of the FitzGeralds of Kildare marked the beginning of the destruction of this once very powerful Old English family. The ensuing 150 years would witness the destruction of many more of the Old English (as those of Anglo-Norman origin were now called) and their replacement by a new Protestant aristocracy. However, all of this was in the future and for the moment the Tudor monarch was much pleased.

In 1536 Wyse was emissary of the city to the royal court at Greenwich. The king presented Wyse with a letter of thanks and a promise of continued royal favour, along with a bearing sword 'to be borne before the mayor from time to time within that our said city'. The sword is on display at Waterford Museum of Treasures and is regarded as one of the finest

The oldest cap of maintenance in Europe, a gift from Henry VIII to William Wyse, mayor of Waterford, 1536.

sixteenth-century swords in either Britain or Ireland. A few weeks later, Wyse was back in Greenwich and again the king pledged his protection of the city's privileges and this time he gave as a gift a cap of maintenance, 'to be borne at times thought fit by you our mayor'. Caps of maintenance were traditionally worn under the crown by the monarch, and during the medieval period they had very special significance. The Waterford cap, made of red velvet from Lucca in Italy and embroidered with Tudor roses and marguerites, was probably made at the royal court. It is the oldest cap of maintenance in Europe and its gift to William Wyse is the first record of the subject of an English monarch being presented with such a gift. It is also the only piece of Henry VIII's wardrobe to survive to the present day.

Henry VIII

The rebellion of the FitzGeralds in Ireland coincided with the English Reformation, which was brought about in part by Henry VIII's desire to divorce Catherine of Aragon and marry Anne Boleyn. The divorce resulted in a break with Rome, which in turn set in motion the dissolution of the monasteries in both England and Ireland. In Ireland the substantial property of the dissolved monasteries was transferred to the landed class in the country and to the merchant class in the cities. Therefore, both Gaelic Irish princes and Anglo-Norman lords profited. In Waterford four monasteries were dissolved. William Wyse had been renting a portion of St John's Priory, the Benedictine monastery. To ensure that no one pipped him to the post, he sent his son, Henry (no doubt named after the king), to Thomas Cromwell, the king's chief minister, with a gift of a 'leish of falcons' and a request for the lands of the dissolved monastery. Having promised to expel the monks, Wyse was given the lands and he took up residence in the old priory, which acquired manorial status. His descendants were known as the Wyses of the Manor of St John.

Wyse was not the only merchant to profit from the dissolution. The Walshs received the property of the Franciscans, but instead of pulling down the old church or converting it to a manor house they established a substantial almshouse known as the Holy Ghost Hospital. Some eight statues dating from the thirteenth century were collected and housed in the almshouse. This is the largest set of medieval statues in Ireland and is now on display at Waterford

Museum of Treasures. In 1544 the almshouse received a charter from the king and 450 years later it is still in existence, though not on the same site.

In 1536 Wyse was made sheriff of County Waterford, a task he carried out with great efficiency. The king's council in Ireland were impressed and reported:

> Mr Wyse of Waterford, the king's servant, a sad, wise, discreet gentlemen ... hath discreetly used himself in that room as he hath trained the people thereabouts to a much better order and obedience than they have been in these many years past.

Wyse was in many ways the last of the great medieval mayors of Waterford. The characteristics that defined the Middle Ages were fading fast. The unity of Christendom had been destroyed by the Reformation, while the death knell of the great Old English lords had been sounded with the destruction of the FitzGeralds, earls of Kildare.

The end of an era

In 1518 the last great episode in the struggle with the town of New Ross took place when 'the citizens and commons of Waterford, together with many Spaniards, Frenchmen, Bretons and Irish, came [to New Ross] riotously with a fleet of boats and ships, in piratical or warlike fashion. They caused much damage to the town and the sovereign and commons of New Ross were compelled to deliver to the mayor and bailiffs of Waterford a mace of silver gilt to the value of twenty pounds.'

The O'Driscolls of Baltimore fared even worse when, on 20 February 1538, four Portuguese ships laden with Spanish wine consigned to the merchants of Waterford were diverted by tempests to Cape Clear and Baltimore. One ship, *La Santa Maria de Soci*, laden with 100 tuns of wine, was driven into the bay adjoining the entrance to the haven of Baltimore. 'Finen O'Driscoll, chieftain of the island ... covenanted with the merchants for three pipes of wine, to conduct the ships safe into the Haven.' However, when the 'Gentry and Peers of those parts had tasted the wine they forgot their promise of safe conduct and inviting the merchants to dinner in the castle, seized and clapped them in irons ... and took the ship, and distributed seventy-two tuns of wine among their neighbours.' On hearing of this action a small fleet was assembled by the men of Waterford to recapture the Portuguese ship and rescue its mariners. However, they recouped only twenty-five of the 100 tuns of wine. The city council decided to teach the O'Driscolls a lesson. The account of the subsequent battle is worth quoting in full.

> On the first day of April the armada set sail, arriving within the Haven of Baltimore by nightfall and anchored towards the castle, which was guarded with men and artillery. They fired at it all night and at the break of day the ward [the garrison] fled and the Waterford men landed in good order in the island [Sherkin Island] and besieged the strong fortress there. The mariners entered the castle by a small port and put up St George's Standard. The army then entered at the Bridge Gate and kept it five days, which they spent in destroying all the villages of the island, and also the house of the Friars Minors near the castle, and the mill of the same. The fortress being double warded by two strong pills or castles with walls and barbicans, the halls, offices, etc., were totally ruined to the ground and tumbled into the sea.
>
> There was found on the island great store of malt, barley and salt. There was taken here Finen O'Driscoll's chief galley of thirty oars, and above three or four score of pinnaces [boats] of which about fifty were burned and the great galley carried to Waterford. Finen had his most pleasant seat in a castle adjoining to a hall, with an orchard and grove, all which they destroyed and razed to the earth, and from thence they entered into another island and burnt all the villages of the same.
>
> Then landing on the mainland they burnt and destroyed Baltimore, and broke down Teig O'Driscoll's goodly castle and bawn. After this on Good Friday the army arrived safely back at Waterford.

Old scores with the long-time enemies of the city had been settled. The power-base of the Baltimore pirates, who had preyed on ships coming to Waterford for two centuries, had finally been destroyed. The port of New Ross would never again pose a serious threat to Waterford's dominance of the harbour. The future seemed very bright for the ruling merchant class of Waterford. However, nothing could have been further from the truth. Religious and political turmoil was about to be unleashed and Waterford would be changed utterly by it.

The Reformation

In January 1547, Henry VIII was succeeded by his nine-year-old son, Edward VI. Under the influence of his uncles and advisers, Edward favoured the consolidation of the English Reformation and in 1549 ordered the *First Book of Common Prayer* to be used in Ireland. However, he reigned for only six years and the religious changes he instigated had little influence on Waterford, although the city, still considered an important outpost of royal authority in Ireland, did receive two new charters from the young king.

Edward was succeeded by his half-sister, Mary, known as Bloody Mary because of her execution of some 400 Protestants in an attempt to restore the Catholic faith in England. In Ireland, Mary introduced the policy of plantation in order to extend the Tudor hold over the country. The plantation of Laois and Offaly marked the beginning of a new strategy of planting loyal English, and later Scottish, settlers on land held by the Irish. Mary also gave Waterford a new charter, the first membrane of which is beautifully illuminated with an image of Mary and her husband, Prince Philip of Spain. (This is on display at Waterford Museum of Treasures.)

During this period Waterford enjoyed a great trade relationship with Spain and most Irish wine imports came from that kingdom. It was these trading links between Waterford merchants and their Spanish and Portuguese counterparts that brought the city into contact with the Catholic teachings of the Counter-Reformation. The failure of the English Reformation and Anglican Church in sixteenth-century Waterford, and indeed in Ireland, was in part due to the success of the Counter-Reformation movement. Among the chief players of this movement were the sons of the city's merchant class, many of whom had been educated in seminaries in Spain, France, Italy and Portugal.

Mary's half-sister, Elizabeth, re-established the (Protestant) Church of England in 1559. For the duration of her long reign the citizens tried to walk a tight rope between showing loyalty to the

queen as head of State and to the pope as head of the
Church. Rejecting State Protestantism, the merchant
class continued to send their sons to the continent to
be educated and trained as priests. Yet on the surface
all appeared well: Elizabeth gave the city a new charter
in 1574 and Sir Henry Sydney, the queen's lord deputy,
visited Waterford in 1567 and was so impressed with the
city that he wrote:

> This city of Waterford much flourisheth and I
> suppose was never in better state since it was
> builted, the people thereof being very civil and full
> of industry.

In 1577 we get the true feeling of the resentment felt by the
merchant class towards the new religion. Dean Cleere, dean of
Christ Church Cathedral and supposedly an upholder of the
Protestant faith, put the silver plate and vestments of Christ
Church Cathedral in the custody of the corporation for a pledge
of £400. This was an ill-disguised attempt to keep these objects
in Catholic hands, reflecting a realisation by the ruling Catholic
merchant class that the Protestant Church was not going away.
Two years later, when the new Protestant bishop of Waterford,
Marmaduke Middleton, tried to impose attendance at divine
service, he stirred up an unholy row that led to the corporation
being fined for non-attendance at Mass and for trying to slander
Middleton.

Decorative panel
from the charter of
Queen Elizabeth I
to the city of
Waterford, 1574.

Ironically, despite these religious tensions, the lord deputy,
Sir William Drury, reported that 'the mayors of Waterford were
the best advisers of foreign news of any town or city in this
land', because they extracted from merchants returning from
Spain evidence of military or naval preparations against England.
However, this was not an age of tolerance and while the merchants
and citizens persisted with the old religion and had their sons trained
as priests in seminaries in Spain, the authorities would not trust
them or accept the concept of dual loyalty. The attempts by the
Catholic King Philip of Spain to invade England in 1588 did little to
endear the Catholics of Ireland to the queen. In 1592 spies reported
that the mayor of Waterford retained in his house a Jesuit seminarian
(the Jesuits were an order of priests who had spearheaded the

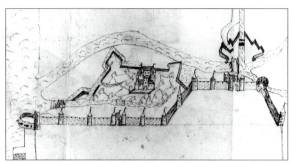

Map of the eastern defences of Waterford, drawn c.1590. Starting at Reginald's Tower, with its blockhouse extending into the River Suir, it continues to the Watch Tower in Railway Square. St John's Bridge and the former Augustinian priory are shown with their relatively recent outer defences clearly marked.

Counter-Reformation movement on the continent), who 'hath at diverse times preached publicly'. The line between politics and religion was now seriously blurred.

In the aftermath of the ill-fated Spanish Armada of 1588, measures were taken to strengthen the defences of the harbour and city. St Patrick's Fort or Citadel was built as an additional defensive structure outside the town wall (parts of it are still visible today). It overlooked the River Suir, yet a near contemporary drawing shows it with cannon facing inwards, towards the city; the queen's officials evidently distrusted the citizens as much as they did the Spanish.

When Elizabeth died in 1603 much of old Ireland had been wiped away and the last of the great Gaelic families had been all but crushed. The way was now paved for the plantation of Ulster, which would begin under her successor, James VI of Scotland, who became James I of England. By the end of Elizabeth's reign very few in the city attended Protestant church service, and on hearing news of her death the citizens, somewhat prematurely, proceeded to restore the public face of Catholicism. Less than two months later lord deputy Mountjoy arrived before the city and the citizens claimed, under the terms of King John's charter (1215), that they had the right to refuse entry even of a royal army. Eventually the citizens submitted to Mountjoy and the Catholic clergy surrendered the churches but were allowed to celebrate Mass in private. King James's administration was much less tolerant than Elizabeth's, and mayors who refused to take the Oath of Supremacy, accepting him as head of the Church, were imprisoned. By 1618 the government's patience ran out as over a period of five years a dozen mayors had been elected and refused the oath. A government official, known as the lord president of Munster, seized the charters and dissolved the corporation.

On the accession of James's son, Charles I, in 1625, the citizens petitioned for a new charter. The king, seriously short of cash, obliged in 1626 in consideration of a fee of £3,000 – an enormous sum of money at that time. It was under the terms of this charter that the city was governed until the Municipal Reform Act of 1840. The charter conferred upon the mayor a new title, that of admiral of the harbour, and his symbol of office became a silver dart. On midsummer's day (21 June), tradition required the mayor to sail downriver and cast the dart into the Meeting of the Waters, that is, where the combined

The fort of Waterford, a late sixteenth-century fort with early seventeenth-century additions, also known as St Patrick's Fort.

rivers Suir, Nore and Barrow meet the sea. In doing so he would drive King Neptune out with the chant: 'According to the Charter, as Mayor of Waterford and Admiral of the Port, I claim these waters.'

However, as far as the majority of the citizens were concerned, King Charles was more of a problem than King Neptune, particularly when it became obvious that Church property would not revert to the Catholics. Though Charles was more tolerant than his father, he too had problems: his adherence to the Church of England was not welcomed by the Puritans in England who also resented his autocratic style and disregard for the institutions of parliament. Despite the reservations of the English parliament with regards to the established Church in both England and Ireland, Charles ordered Thomas Wentworth, his lord deputy in Ireland, to reform the Church of Ireland (the Protestant or Anglican Church in Ireland). In Waterford this meant the return of the silver plate and vestments that had been given to the corporation by dean Cleere in 1577. The letter sent by Wentworth to the mayor demanding their return has survived and, by a miracle of good fortune, so have the vestments. Thankfully, on their return to the now Protestant cathedral the vestments were hidden, and so when the cathedral was sacked by the Cromwellians in 1650 they were left intact. The vestments were not recovered until 1773 (see Christ Church Cathedral in part two) and are now on display at Waterford Museum of Treasures. Wentworth returned to England and fell out of favour with parliament. In an attempt to placate parliament, Charles assented to his execution in 1641, but not before the unfortunate Wentworth advised his fellow Englishmen to 'put not their faith in princes'.

For God, King and Fatherland

In 1641 a great rebellion broke out in Ireland, which saw the massacre of the Protestant planters who had settled in Ulster during the reign of James I. Protestant communities outside Ulster were also plundered. It was during these disturbances that the city of Waterford admitted the Irish army of lord Mountgarret, and for the next seven years, until it fell to Cromwell's parliamentary army in 1650, the city remained in Catholic hands.

Waterford city had now joined forces with the Confederate Catholics of Ireland. Their motto was *Pro Deo, Rege et Patria* – For God, King and Fatherland. The confederation's aim was to administer the Catholic-controlled parts of the country pending a final settlement with the king. Representatives of this alliance of Old Irish, Old English and some new English met mainly at Kilkenny, though they also met occasionally at Waterford. The printing press of the confederation was based in Waterford, Thomas Burke being the printer (a copy of one of his publications is on display in Waterford Museum of Treasures). In time the confederation split into various factions and the whole matter was further complicated by the outbreak of civil war in England. The confederates sought to obtain from the king some measure of religious tolerance, in return the king expected support against the English parliament.

At this time Waterford, with its commercial and religious links with Spain, France and Italy, was known as *Parva Roma* (Little Rome). The leading citizens' loyalty to the papacy ensured that in negotiations with the king's government the city would only support full restitution of the Catholic Church in Ireland. It is easy to understand the depth of feeling in the city when we recall that many of the leading players in the Counter-Reformation in Ireland had Waterford connections.

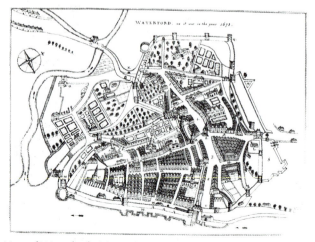

Map of Waterford, 1673.

The Counter-Reformation

Waterford-born Peter Lombard (1554–1625), archbishop of Armagh and senior Catholic prelate in Ireland, was the major Irish figure of the Counter-Reformation. In 1595 he acted as the representative, in Rome, of Hugh O'Neill, the last great hope of Gaelic Ireland. Thus a potent figure of the Old English faction in Ireland championed the cause of the foremost Gaelic Irish chieftain. Lombard encouraged the Irish to support O'Neill, promising the same privileges and indulgences as were granted to the crusaders to the Holy Land. The importance of the role Lombard played in Irish affairs can be gauged from a speech made by James I to parliament, in which he accused the Irish of being only 'half subjects'. He placed much of the blame for this situation on Doctor Peter Lombard in Rome, who, he said, 'makes the Catholics send their sons to seminaries in Spain, France, Italy and the Netherlands, who when they return act as traitors'.

When O'Neill surrendered in 1603 following the failed Spanish invasion, Lombard, always a realist, argued for the acceptance of James as king if he granted religious tolerance to Catholics. The king, however, was not disposed to compromise. In the end, Lombard tried to come to terms with the political reality and was among the first of the leading churchmen to preach the notion of reaching an accommodation with the new Protestant states.

Though less well known, Lombard's fellow citizen, William Lee, was also paving the way for the success of the Counter-Reformation when, in 1578, he established an Irish College in Paris. Luke Wadding, another son of Waterford, founded St Isidore's College in Rome and in time would fill Lombard's shoes as Ireland's representative at the Vatican. Under Wadding's influence, Irish Franciscan colleges were founded throughout Europe.

On the political front, Wadding was subsequently appointed Roman agent to the confederation. He encouraged Pope Innocent X to send Cardinal Rinuccini to meet with the confederate Catholics. Unfortunately for the Irish and Old English, the negotiations with the king came to nothing because in January 1649 King Charles I was executed by a Puritan-dominated parliament, which was to appoint Oliver Cromwell governor general of Ireland a few months later.

The   Reformation   and   Counter-Reformation,   the

Silver chalice with the inscription (in Latin): 'Geoffrey Keating had me made 1634'.

destruction of the Gaelic princes, the decline in the fortunes of many of the Old English families and the plantations brought into question what it was to be Irish. The man who best answered this and articulated a concept of Irishness was Geoffrey Keating, whose great work *Foras Feasa ar Eirinn* (*A History of Ireland from the Earliest Times*) was written in the first half of the seventeenth century. His interpretation of his world offered contemporaries and later readers a sense of Ireland, of Irishness and of Catholicism that had wide appeal. He inspired later generations and ensured that the culture of Gaelic Ireland and indeed that of the Old English would not be lost, but would survive the religious wars that so blighted Ireland in the seventeenth century. Geoffrey Keating, the most influential writer of his time, was a priest of the dioceses of Waterford and Lismore, and a magnificent silver chalice he commissioned in 1634 is on display at Waterford Museum of Treasures.

Cromwell at the gates

Keating's defence of Catholic Ireland would cut no slack with Oliver Cromwell, who set sail for Ireland in August 1649. Cromwell claimed that the southern ports were his primary objective, fearing that they were the most likely to give succour to the late king's supporters. He landed at Ringsend in Dublin and marched north to Drogheda where there was a massacre of the townspeople, carried out both as an object lesson to others who might resist and in revenge for the massacre of Protestants in the 1641 rebellion. The townspeople of Wexford fared no better when he finally decided to march south, and when New Ross surrendered Cromwell informed the townspeople that 'where the parliament of England has power Mass will not be allowed'.

By 24 November Cromwell's army was outside the gates of Waterford. The siege lasted nine days. However, the absence of artillery, bad weather, an outbreak of dysentery among his troops and the need to find winter quarters forced Cromwell to raise the siege. On 2 December the army marched away; Cromwell described it as 'so terrible a day as ever I marched in all my life'.

Cromwell departed Ireland in 1650 and left his son-in-law, Ireton, in command of the besieging army, and in August that year Waterford surrendered to him. A cannon ball from this siege of the city is still embedded in the wall of Reginald's Tower, a potent reminder of those terrible times. In London, parliament ordered a day of thanksgiving to celebrate the fall of Waterford and notices were posted about the city informing the citizens. Only one of these proclamations has survived and can be seen at Waterford Museum of Treasures.

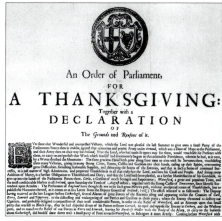

The English parliament proclaims a day of thanksgiving to be held on 30 August 1650 to celebrate the fall of Waterford to parliamentary forces.

The fall of the city was followed by what can only be described as a policy of ethnic cleansing. Hoards of homeless people were now wandering the countryside and the towns, and when apprehended they were shipped off to Barbados as indentured servants to the English planters. (To this day there is a small village in Barbados called Waterford.) Many of the city's merchant class were also driven out and, theoretically, no Catholics were allowed within the town walls. In the census of 1659 we find over half the tax-paying households within the walled town were in the hands of newly arrived English planters. However, when the suburbs were taken into account the planters were outnumbered in a ratio of about two to three.

The Restoration

Cromwell died in 1658 and the problem of succession was finally resolved when the monarchy was restored in 1660. However, the new king, Charles II, was in a no-win situation as far as the dispossessed Irish Catholics were concerned. Petitions to the king from both the Catholic merchant class still residing in Waterford and those now living abroad came to nothing. If he were he to reinstate their lands and property, he would face certain revolt from the parliamentary faction. As a result, the Irish Catholics found the gates to their own land and houses still barred against them.

Both Catholics and non-conformists in Waterford were greatly resented by the new corporation, which hoped to keep their numbers to a minimum. It should be remembered however that the new ruling class felt very insecure because not only were they in a minority, but its members had also conspired against the monarchy. William Bolton, one of the leading Cromwellian figures in Waterford and mayor of the city in 1662, had to perform a complete about-face when the monarchy was restored and apply to the king for a pardon and confirmation of his lands at Faithlegg in County Waterford. (The original pardon and confirmation of lands are on display at Waterford Museum of Treasures.) The Faithlegg property had been given to him in recognition of services rendered to the Cromwellian regime. The land had belonged to the Aylwards, who were evicted and transported to Connaught, like many other Catholic families. Thus was born the slogan: 'To Hell or Connaught'. It is an interesting quirk of history that the Aylwards, originally Bristol merchants, had acquired these lands as payment for supplying the ships that transported King Henry II to Ireland in 1171.

Late seventeenth-century image of King James II's departure from Ireland in 1690.

Only in the dying years of Charles II's reign do we find a more tolerant attitude prevailing, and several Catholics were admitted as freemen of Waterford, a privilege that allowed them trade as merchants. Upon Charles's death the Catholic James II became king of England. The city received a new charter, and in the new city council Catholics were now in a majority. However, within five years William of Orange had defeated James at the Battle of the Boyne and the Protestant ascendancy was restored. Following his defeat, James fled to Waterford from where he took a ship to Kinsale and then on to exile in France. Local tradition holds that before he set sail from Waterford he climbed to the top of Reginald's Tower to take a last look at his lost kingdom. James was destined to be the last Catholic monarch of England, Ireland and Scotland. Though William of Orange, the new king of England, promised the Catholic inhabitants of Waterford that they would not be molested in their properties, the early decades of the eighteenth century proved difficult for them.

An age of elegance: the eighteenth century

During the eighteenth century Protestants controlled the Dublin parliament, and in the early 1700s a series of laws was enacted designed to exclude both Catholics and non-conformists from public life. Civic office was closed to them as was any position that would enable them to accumulate wealth. Yet despite these impediments, and the fact that the corporation was exclusively Protestant, some steps were taken that showed a level of religious tolerance. In 1704 the corporation dropped commercial restrictions against Catholics and others, although the minutes record that the motive was 'the great decay of trade in this city'. The promotion of the city over individual self-interest was again noted in 1727 when the members of the corporation agreed to relinquish their claim on import taxes, even though they personally would have benefited from them. In the same year twelve persons were accepted as freemen of Waterford, four of whom were Catholics. The admittance of Catholics as freemen was something that had begun as early as 1710. In spite of the oppressive religious laws, in the first half of the century Waterford had meeting houses for Quakers, Presbyterians and Baptists, and in 1745 it housed three Catholic churches.

Many of the Catholic merchant class who were driven abroad in the post-Cromwellian period found refuge in Catholic Spain and France because of their previous contacts with the wine trade there. In time these families prospered and their descendants endowed the churches in Waterford with rich gifts of silver devotional objects, some of which are on display in Waterford Museum of Treasures.

The eighteenth century saw huge changes in the very fabric of the city, reflecting both the wealth and confidence of the new ruling class. As early as 1696 work began on the demolition of the city's medieval defences. Along the quay, often using the base of the old wall as a foundation, the new merchant class built their homes overlooking the River Suir. These were tall three- and four-storey houses that had, after the Dutch fashion, their gables to the front and were known as Dutch Billies. This style of building was introduced by Dutch settlers who were fleeing from religious persecution on

The Exchange at Waterford by John Thomas Serres (1759–1825). The Exchange was built between 1710 and 1714 and occupied the site of the present Ulster Bank on the quay.

the continent and were encouraged by William of Orange to settle in Ireland. Also built on the quay was the Exchange, completed in 1714, where the corporation met and the merchants transacted business. As early as 1703 a piped water system was in operation in the city, and in 1732 street lighting was installed and a special system of rating householders was devised to cover the maintenance costs.

The pace of change was quite staggering. What we know today as the Mall was created in the 1730s when the Pill or St John's River was diverted and the area it occupied reclaimed. Rows of very fashionable elm trees were planted to make a pleasant walkway, and opposite Reginald's Tower a bowling-green was laid out. The French Hugue-nots – Protestant refugee settlers who were invited to the city in 1693 by King William – brought this fashion to Waterford. The beauty of the city's quayside was eulogised by the historian Charles Smith in 1746 when he wrote:

> It is above half a mile in length and of considerable breadth, is not inferior to, but rather exceeds the most celebrated in Europe. The Exchange, Custom House and other public buildings, besides the houses of the merchants and citizens ranged along the quay, are no small addition to its beauty.

Smith was not alone in his admiration; in 1736 the city council commissioned the Dutch artist Van der Hagen, the father of Irish landscape painting, to capture on canvas the vista that the new settlers had created along the quay. Today the painting, the earliest view of an Irish city, hangs in the council chamber at City Hall.

View of Waterford, 1736, by William Van der Hagen.

In the early 1740s the Church of Ireland bishop Charles Este commissioned the renowned German architect Richard Castle (1695–1751) to build a new palace. Castle also has to his credit some of the finest houses in Ireland, including Powerscourt in County Wicklow and Carton in County Kildare. Instead of facing inwards, as the old palace did, he positioned the new building so that its back

was to the cathedral. He also demolished part of the old town wall to
create a terraced garden in front of
the palace, which overlooked the
newly created Mall. The Bishop's
Palace reflected the vision of the
outward-looking, expansionary city
and paved the way for even greater
change. The man who masterminded
these later changes, transforming the

An 1812 view of the Bishop's Palace, City Hall
and the Mall by Samuel Frederick Brocas.

medieval city into an eighteenth-century European city, was John
Roberts, a member of the Church of Ireland. Among other fine buildings, Roberts has to his credit the Church of Ireland cathedral
(1773), City Hall (1783) and the Roman Catholic cathedral (1796) –
the first built in either Britain or Ireland after the Reformation.

It was trade and commerce that fuelled this building boom, and
for much of the eighteenth century Waterford was the third busiest
port in Ireland. One of the most important trade routes was that with
Newfoundland in North America, and by 1770 the route absorbed
between ten and fifteen percent of the city's exports. Not only did the
city's merchants provision the English ships sailing to Newfoundland
for the fishing season, but Waterford fishermen and mariners found
much-needed employment there also, travelling seasonally from the
second half of the seven-
teenth century onwards.
In the second half of the
nineteenth century this
became a wave of perma-
nent emigration. An esti-
mated   30,000–35,000
people, drawn overwhelm-
ingly from Waterford and

View of Waterford from Ryland's *History of Waterford,*
published 1824.

its hinterland, settled in Newfoundland between 1800 and 1830; this
represents the largest pre-Famine exodus from Ireland. The Waterford origins of the emigrants has given Newfoundland's culture and
spoken English a distinctive flavour, and even to this day that state's
inhabitants, although separated by the Atlantic Ocean, still speak
with an unmistakable Waterford accent.

Glass-making

Among the merchant class that profited from the provisioning of this lucrative fishing industry was the Penroses, a Quaker family that had settled in Waterford during the late seventeenth century. The changing political climate on the other side of the Atlantic led the Penroses to establish their now world-famous glass factory in Waterford. The American War of Independence inspired the Irish parliament to demand free trade from the Imperial parliament in London. Fearing that Ireland might go the same way as the newly formed United States, the London parliament made concessions in 1780 which allowed Irish merchants to trade freely with the colonies and also to export both wool and glass. Within three years of the lifting of the restriction on glass-making, George Penrose, together with his nephew, William, had established a glass factory. The Penroses knew much about commerce, marketing and profit margins, but little about glass-making. Something of the anxiety felt by the family about their new investment is beautifully captured in verse by Rachel Penrose, William's wife, who penned in her diary:

Early nineteenth-century cut-glass table centrepiece made at the Waterford glass-house.

My Billy's mind oft full of care
He to the fire turns his chair
And thus by him I'm oft addressed
My Jewel what does thee think best
Of money matters and provisions
Of business in each division
Of Glass House and of this man's order
Of such a glass and such a border
Decanters goblets and of crofts
And of new warehouses and the loftes.

In order to produce high-quality glassware they recruited craftsmen from Stourbridge in England, which had been a major centre of glass production since the sixteenth century. The Penroses then chose another Quaker, John Hill, already an important glass-maker, to manage the glass-house. Hill's decision to bring his skills to the city was one of the most important factors in the birth of Waterford's glass-making tradition.

Hill, whose knowledge of glass chemistry, quality, style and design became the key to the success of the enterprise, was to leave the company after only three years' service. It appears that Rachel Penrose, the wife of his employer, made an accusation against him. In a letter to Jonathan Gatchell, a clerk at the glass-house, John Hill set down his bitter feelings about the situation:

> It is impossible for me to express the feeling of my poor mind when I acquaint thee that I am obliged to leave this kingdom [Ireland], my reasons I need not tell thee, but I sincerely wish I had been made acquainted with the base ingratitude of the worst of villains sooner and probably then I may have remedied it, but now 'tis too late ...

As a parting shot, Hill left the secret formula for making clear glass, which was the keystone of Penroses's success, to Gatchell. Under Gatchell's supervision, first as compounder, then as partner and subsequently as owner, there was an outpouring of crystal glassware that utilised the most elaborate cutting and engraving techniques. There were numerous accolades for the Waterford glass-house, the most noteworthy an invitation to show at the Great Exhibition in London in 1851. In Waterford Museum of Treasures there is a magnificent display of early Waterford glass, representing the epitome of Irish and Waterford glass, which glass designers in England, Bohemia, America and even Japan followed in the early nineteenth century.

Ship-building

By the mid-nineteenth century the Penrose family was no longer involved in glass-making, having acquired one of the three ship-building works in the city. The Neptune shipyard, one of their rivals, was owned by the Malcomsons, also Quakers. It was from the Neptune shipyard that, in 1846, a ship called the *SS Neptune* was launched. This ship had the honour of inaugurating the London–St Petersburg service. As the *SS Neptune* steamed up the Neva River she was greeted by His Imperial Majesty Czar Nicholas I who decreed that the ship be freed for all time from all port dues. In return the Czar was presented with a suite of Waterford glass.

This was the great age of ship-building in Waterford. Some forty steamers were built at the Neptune yard, all of them for Malcomson

Brothers, who held the largest fleet of iron steamers in the world from the mid-1850s to the late 1860s. There were five transatlantic passenger liners built at Waterford for the Malcomson-owned London–Le Harve–New York line. No doubt these ships took some of the million or more souls that were forced to flee the Famine in the 1840s and 1850s, in search of a new life in either Britain or America. There is little in Waterford today to remind us of these departures or indeed of this great ship-building tradition. However, in the foyer of Waterford Museum of Treasures stands a huge stock anchor, one of a set of six used to launch ships from the Neptune yard in the mid-nineteenth century.

In the eighteenth and early nineteenth century, Quakers made up only about two percent of the population in Waterford, yet their contribution to the city was immense. Families like the Penroses and the Malcomsons became involved in industry partly because, being non-conformists, they, like Catholics, were restricted by the Penal Laws, which excluded them from public life and land ownership.

The struggle for Catholic emancipation had occupied the Catholic gentry since these discriminating laws came into force in the late seventeenth and early eighteenth century. Chief among the eighteenth-century Catholic gentry in Waterford who were active in the quest for religious freedom was Thomas Wyse (1701–1770), a direct descendant of William Wyse, who had received the sword, cap of maintenance and St John's monastery from Henry VIII many centuries earlier. The Wyses of the Manor of St John had achieved the remarkable feat of holding on to their estates and evading the rigours of the Penal Laws whilst openly remaining true to their Catholic religion. The Penal Laws demanded the division of land among all the sons in a family, thus over a period of a few generations those landed Catholic families who had escaped being dispossessed during the seventeenth century would find their power and influence diminish as their estate was subdivided by each succeeding generation. The Penal Laws also demanded that if one son became a Protestant then the estate automatically went to him. The Wyse family of Waterford, against all the odds, particularly biological, managed to retain their estate intact because each generation produced only one surviving male heir, thus preventing subdivision and removing the temptation to adopt the Protestant faith.

Thomas Wyse, a Catholic landowner, was known locally as

Bullocks Wyse due to his habit of harnessing a team of prize bullocks to draw his carriage through the streets of Waterford; Catholics were forbidden to own a horse worth more than £5. This larger-than-life character even had the temerity to remove one of the medieval gates to the city because it restricted access to his property, which stood outside the city walls. One Sunday morning, Wyse rounded up his estate workers and while the city officials were at service in Christ Church Cathedral he had the gate removed. Wyse's son, John, built Newtown House in Waterford in the 1780s as the new family residence, almost certainly designed by John Roberts. When John Wyse went bankrupt in 1796 the house was sold to the Quakers and a school was set up there in 1798. The multi-denominational school still operates today and boasts a fine reputation throughout Ireland.

Reform and Rebellion

Bullocks Wyse's great-grandson, Thomas, later Sir Thomas, was, like many of his ancestors, a larger-than-life character and he played a leading role in the nineteenth-century campaign for Catholic emancipation. The first major step on the road to emancipation was in 1826 when Daniel O'Connell (known as The Liberator) personally joined the election campaign of Henry Villiers-Stuart. Villiers-Stuart was a County Waterford Protestant landlord who supported Catholic emancipation, and his election to the parliament at Westminster broke the power of the sitting MP and landlord who opposed it. Thomas Wyse played a leading part in this campaign and was instrumental in ensuring the success of Villiers-Stuart. About a month after the election, O'Connell, inspired by the determination of the County Waterford tenantry, installed in the city the first members of his Order of Liberators. Two years later O'Connell, a Catholic, was himself elected MP for Clare, and in 1829, faced with the dilemma of refusing to admit him to the House of Commons, the British parliament passed the Roman Catholic Relief Act. In 1830 O'Connell took his seat in parliament – Catholic

Presentation Convent, built in 1842.

emancipation had been achieved. The following year O'Connell was returned MP for Waterford city.

Thomas Wyse was also elected MP for Waterford (1835–1847) and following O'Connell's success he wrote a history of the Catholic Association. He did not support O'Connell's Repeal Movement however, which called for the restoration of the Irish parliament. Instead he became involved in educational reform and was one of the commissioners for the building of the new Houses of Parliament at Westminster in London. The architect commissioned was the famous Augustus Welby Pugin, who became acquainted with Wyse and designed his new Manor of St John at Lisduggan, in the suburbs of Waterford. Pugin also designed the nearby Presentation convent, one of his most convincing buildings. Built in the style of a medieval monastery, the convent is complete with round tower and covered cloister. Wyse was made British minister to the new kingdom of Greece, which, for a short time, he virtually ruled. He married Napoleon's niece, Letitia Bonaparte, and was knighted in 1856. When he died in 1862 the Greek government gave him a State funeral. During his distinguished life he brought a breath of internationalism to Waterford.

Early photograph of Thomas Meagher, mayor of Waterford, 1843–1844.

In the 1840s, Daniel O'Connell worked for the restoration of the Irish parliament, which had been closed when the Act of Union (1800) united the parliaments of Britain and Ireland. Catholics were now gaining confidence and political experience as the Irish Municipal Reform Act (1840) brought more democracy to local government and Catholics began to dominate many of the country's city councils. In Waterford in 1843, Thomas Meagher, the Newfoundland-born son of an emigrant, was elected mayor of Waterford – the first Catholic to hold the title since the seventeenth century. Thanks to the Newfoundland fishing industry, Meagher was a very wealthy merchant and he became a staunch supporter of O'Connell's Repeal Movement.

The failure of the Repeal Movement to reinstate the Irish parliament caused many of the younger members to break away and form a group known as the Young Irelanders. In 1846, as the Great Famine

raged, the Repeal Move-
ment split between O'Con-
nellites   and   Young
Irelanders, one of whom
was   Thomas   Francis
Meagher, son of the mayor
of Waterford and known as
Meagher of the Sword. The
following year was known
as Black '47, when hun-
dreds of thousands per-
ished as a direct or indirect
result of the Famine, and
the leader of Catholic Ireland,   Daniel   O'Connell,

The Granville Hotel, c.1900, birthplace of
Thomas Francis Meagher.

died in Rome. In 1848 the Young Irelanders staged a rebellion, but it
was a failure and Meagher and the other leaders were arrested and
tried for treason. Meagher was sentenced to be hanged, drawn and
quartered, however this was later commuted to transportation to
Van Diemen's Land (Australia) for life.

In   1856   Meagher   escaped   from
Van Diemen's Land and went to America where
he played a role in the civil war, founding the
Irish Brigade. During the civil war, the bloodi-
est battles for Meagher's Irish Brigade were at
Antietam in September 1862 and at Fredericksburg in December 1862. Thanks to the gal-
lantry of Meagher's men at Antietam Creek,
the gravest threat to the Union was checked.
At Fredericksburg, Virginia, where over 5,000
men were either killed or wounded, General
Robert E Lee, the confederate colonel-in-chief,
declared that never were men so brave as

Lithograph of Thomas Francis
Meagher, signed and dated 1848.

Meagher's Irish Brigade. Meagher's leadership, bravery and gal-
lantry, and that of his men, did much to ensure the Union victory.

After the war the president appointed Meagher as acting governor
of Montana. This very colourful man, who had played such an important role in the history of Ireland and in his adopted country the
United States, died in 1867. In 1886 his widow presented to the city

of Waterford a large framed portrait of Meagher, together with regi-
mental flags, civil war swords and medals and a tunic. These objects
are now on display at Waterford Museum of Treasures.

Nineteenth-century Waterford

In the years following the Great Famine emigration to Britain,
Canada and the United States continued to drain the country of its
young people. While the city provided employment in ship-building,
brewing, bacon-curing and other agriculture-related industries,
there would never be enough jobs to provide employment for the
thousands that fled rural areas each year. The nineteenth century
was peculiar in that the apparent prosperity of the port was not
matched by rising standards of living among the poor of the city. This
was an era when many of the rich merchants, professionals and indus-
trialists took to living outside the city in fine mansions overlooking
the River Suir or in the airier properties in the suburbs. As they
vacated the city centre the Georgian houses and streets in the older
parts of the city became slums where people lived in the most appall-
ing and overcrowded conditions.

Arundel Square c.1890, showing the tower of Blackfriars in the background.

An already grave situation was exacerbated by a rising population, due mainly to the growing number of homeless people from the country who sought work and shelter in the city from the 1830s onwards. The merchant class did not completely ignore the plight of their poorer fellow citizens, and many almshouses were established to help them, indeed Waterford was quite exceptional in the nineteenth century in that regard. However, it was the charitable work of the Callan-born Waterford merchant Edmund Ignatius Rice that had the most enduring impact. In 1803 Rice founded a school for poor boys of the city, and by 1823 there were some 600 boys receiving a free education at Mount Sion School in Barrack Street. From these small beginnings there grew the worldwide organisation known as the Irish Christian Brothers. Brother Rice is buried in a specially dedicated chapel at Mount Sion, and in the adjoining monastery a very interesting museum is dedicated to his memory.

Yet all was not doom and gloom in nineteenth-century Waterford. The reformed corporation, which had elected Thomas Meagher as mayor in 1843, erected a new, neo-classical courthouse in 1849 on the site of the medieval St Catherine's Abbey. In 1857, in the vicinity of the courthouse, the corporation initiated a drainage scheme, diverting St John's River in order

Waterford's busy quay, c.1900.

to create the People's Park, which to this day provides a welcome retreat for the citizens. The busy quayside got its own timepiece with the building of the clock tower, one of the best- known landmarks in the city. Built in 1861 at a cost of £200, the Gothic-style granite and limestone clock provided a useful social amenity both for the wayfarer and the local community.

By 1900 Waterford was again playing a central role in national politics when the MP for the city, John Redmond, was elected leader of the newly united Home Rule Party, which had split in 1890 following the Charles Stewart Parnell divorce scandal. In 1911 work was begun on a new bridge over the River Suir to replace Timbertoes, the bridge that had been erected in 1793. The new bridge was completed in 1913 and opened by Redmond, after whom it was named. There was a great air of optimism in the city at this time because a year earlier, in 1912, the House of Commons in London had passed the third Irish Home Rule Bill. The House of Lords had rejected it, but as they could only delay it for two years nationalists in Ireland were confident that by late 1914 Ireland would have its parliament restored and John Redmond would be the first prime minister. However, the First World War intervened and the setting up of the Dublin parliament was put on hold. By the time the war was over, in 1918, Redmond was dead and the 1916 Rising had changed nationalist opinion in favour of an independent republic and not simply home rule. In the 1918 general election, Redmond's Home Rule party was defeated and Ireland was plunged into a war of Independence that was followed by a bloody civil war.

Ballybricken, *c.*1900, the Irishtown of Waterford city and home, since the seventeenth century, of the city's livestock market.

Urban renewal

The development of Waterford city in the twentieth century mirrors that of Ireland as a whole. The difficulties for any small post-colonial economy are well documented. Historically, the city depended on servicing its rich agricultural hinterland. Problems of access to the British market, followed by the isolations of the Second World War played havoc with traditional industry and commerce and with the local economy. The period after the war saw the creation of a more open and vigorous Ireland, keen to develop and integrate its economy into the larger European and world markets. The development of Waterford Crystal in this period was an important catalyst for change, and has since been established as one of the most famous brand names in the world. At the end of the twentieth century, over 350,000

St John's River and the waterside, c.1929 (Fr Browne Collection).

visitors per year make the trip to the Crystal Gallery and Workshops, making Waterford one of Ireland's top tourist destinations.

Waterford has been fortunate to benefit from Ireland's industrial, tourism and commercial expansion. Its excellent location and port facilities have enabled the city to fully partake in the growth in the Irish economy. The city is home to a very wide range of international companies in the pharmaceutical, financial services, healthcare, computer, engineering and software sectors, which occupy one of the largest Industrial Development Authority parks in the country. These modern industries blend in seamlessly with more traditional industries, such as food-processing, light engineering, glass-making, brewing, transport and retail. Tourism plays an increasingly important role in the city economy. The development of the international cruise-line business in the past decade brings a regular stream of liners to the city in the summer months. It has brought a new dimension to the local tourist trade and has underlined the importance of the river and the quay frontage of the city.

As in the eighteenth century, the late twentieth century saw unprecedented urban renewal take place in Waterford. A new heart was transplanted into the old core to facilitate retail redevelopment. Prior to the work, the entire site was archaeologically excavated, a huge project that took nearly six years. The archaeologists peeled back the layers of the fifteenth, fourteenth, thirteenth, twelfth and eleventh centuries to Viking Age Waterford. The objects recovered, many of national and international importance, were carefully conserved. A new museum, Waterford Treasures, was opened to display these artefacts and other precious objects from the city's archives and treasury.

In the process of urban renewal, it was decided that the physical layout of old Waterford, caught in an elbow between the quays and the tree-lined, eighteenth-century Mall, would facilitate a major pedestrian zone in the city centre. Since 1986 cars have been excluded from much of the city centre and the impressive John Roberts Square has been designed and laid out to much national critical acclaim.

Redmond Bridge.

The quay remains Waterford's window on the world. In the last decades of the twentieth century major growth in shipping traffic demanded that the port move to a new purpose-built facility at Belview, five miles downstream. This decision, combined with the wider thrust of urban renewal, triggered the renaissance of the city. Following the downstream move of the port, the decision was taken to remove the sheds and warehouses of the working port, which lined the south quays of the city. The building of a riverside walk along the quay frontage, away from noise and traffic, was also undertaken. This walk is now very popular and follows the river to the new William Vincent Wallace Plaza, and on to the Adelphi Quay, Scotts Quay and Canada Street areas.

William Vincent Wallace Plaza, opposite Reginald's Tower, was built by Waterford Corporation to celebrate the new millennium. It honours in name the nineteenth-century operatic composer who was born in nearby Colbeck Street. The plaza incorporates the best in modern Irish design and town-planning and is regarded as one of the finest open-air performance spaces in Ireland, ideally located as it is near the new yacht marina. At the eastern end of the plaza the twin ships' prows in limestone commemorate the tragic loss of the Waterford Shipping Company's steamers, *Formby* and *Conningbeg*, in December 1917.

Successive government reports have selected Waterford as the economic growth centre of the southeast region. This led to the establishment of Waterford Institute of Technology (WIT) in 1970. WIT is now one of the largest colleges in the third-level sector, catering for more than 10,000 full-time and part-time students to post-graduate level in schools of engineering, science, humanities and business. The college is deeply involved in research and development programmes and has been chosen as the focus for expansion of degree-level education in the southeast region. WIT has established a vibrant youth population and has made a major contribution to the economic, social, cultural and sporting life of the city.

Waterford Regional Hospital (WRH) was established in 1987 as the major acute facility for the southeast region. It houses a specialist medical teaching facility of the Royal College of Surgeons of Ireland, and employs over 2,000 medical and paramedical personnel. The hospital is being developed as a 650-bed unit, offering all necessary regional specialities. State-of-the-art orthopaedics, oncology,

CT, magnetic imaging and other services are being developed, reinforcing the city's role as regional capital.

The economic success of Ireland in the late twentieth century was such that it could no longer be classed as a poorer region and therefore could not benefit under Objective One Status from EU financing. In the subsequent realignment of regional boundaries, Waterford city was chosen as the location for the assembly and headquarters of the southern and eastern region, which includes Dublin and Cork. Monthly meetings of this important regional assembly take place in the beautifully restored Assembly House in O'Connell Street.

The modern city

The age profile of Waterford, with a huge population bulge in the under-twenty-five age group, ensures a lively social and cultural scene. Youth-oriented pubs, restaurants, eateries of all kinds and night clubs tend to be concentrated around the Applemarket and John Street area. The older age group is well catered for in High Street/the Mall area with an excellent choice of traditional and ethnic restaurants and pubs. This is a city where there is something for everyone.

The beautifully restored eighteenth-century performance area in the Large Room of the City Hall hosts the annual chamber music winter season of Waterford Music Club and a wide variety of other classical and traditional performances, including the summer season Waterford Show. This is well worth a visit and gives a theatrical overview of Waterford through the ages. The music department at the Institute of Technology also runs a huge variety of musical events, including the Waterford New Music Festival each February, in their college chapel at the Good Shepherd campus on College Street. An annual season of symphonic music, featuring regional, national and international orchestras, is held in the institute's college hall at their Cork Road campus. The Waterford International Festival of Light Opera, which takes place each autumn, is a showcase for musical talent of this particular genre.

The city has three theatres – the Forum, Garter Lane and Theatre Royal – offering a wide range of performances. The Theatre Royal is a beautiful nineteenth-century theatre on the site of an eighteenth-

The *Hanseatic*, an 8,000-tonne German cruise ship, at Waterford, with the Granville Hotel in the background.

century playhouse. It is one of the last surviving Victorian theatres of its type and is well maintained. Garter Lane showcases all manner of productions, from visual arts exhibitions, literary events, such as the Sean Dunne Weekend, to arthouse cinema, poetry readings, dance, music and theatre for all tastes. Waterford's nationally acclaimed professional theatre group, Red Kettle, perform regularly at all the venues in the city. They have a policy of commissioning and premiering new work. Other groups with regular performances in the city include the amateur Waterford Dramatic Society, Young Red Kettle and Waterford Youth Drama.

The highlight of the summer outdoor season is the annual *Spraoi* carnival held over the August bank holiday weekend. This spectacle draws thousands of people, and especially family groups, to the city. The entertainment is widespread and street-based, and admission to most events is free. The culmination of the weekend festivities is a huge street parade and fireworks display. During the summer months, Artbite promotes a series of (usually free) outdoor cultural events, music, live performance, etc, at various sites around the city centre. The corporation has developed a site at Greyfriars as a public gallery space and it houses Waterford's municipal art collection.

The future of Waterford city was never as bright. New road networks are ending the difficulties of intra- and inter-regional travel. The Second River-Crossing, plus the Northern Bypass, Western Bypass and Outer Ring Road will remove much of the burden of heavy traffic from the old city centre. The new motorway from Waterford to Dublin and investment in rail access and in Waterford Regional Airport will create a new dynamic in travel from Waterford to Dublin and further afield. The recent development of a dedicated eighty-acre Technology Park, designed to cater for international financial services and companies in the software and hi-tech sector, has also been a huge boost. The removal of the last remnants of port activity from the quays and wharfs at the north side of the River Suir will enable the development of this spectacular site to go ahead. The population continues to grow steadily, with that of the city and its immediate hinterland expected to reach 100,000 within the next decade. Looking around busy, thriving Waterford today, one is reminded of the comment made by the lord deputy of Ireland in 1567:

> The city of Waterford is much flourisheth and I suppose was never been in a better state since it was built, the people there being very civil and full of industry.

...ok Lighthouse at the entrance to Waterford harbour, built *c.*1215 by William Marshall, lord of Leinster and husband of Isobel, the daughter of Strongbow and Aoife.

The quays in Waterford were described by eighteenth-century commentators as one of the noblest quay areas in Europe.

A Viking ship ferries the mayor and members of Waterford City Council to the opening of Waterford Museum of Treasures, May 1999.

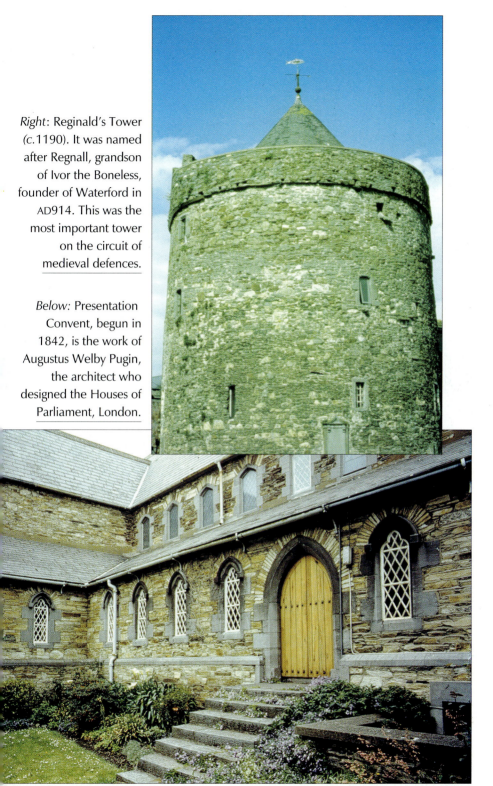

Right: Reginald's Tower (*c.*1190). It was named after Regnall, grandson of Ivor the Boneless, founder of Waterford in AD914. This was the most important tower on the circuit of medieval defences.

Below: Presentation Convent, begun in 1842, is the work of Augustus Welby Pugin, the architect who designed the Houses of Parliament, London.

William Vincent Wallace Plaza by day and by night.

A nineteenth-century bridge over St John's River.

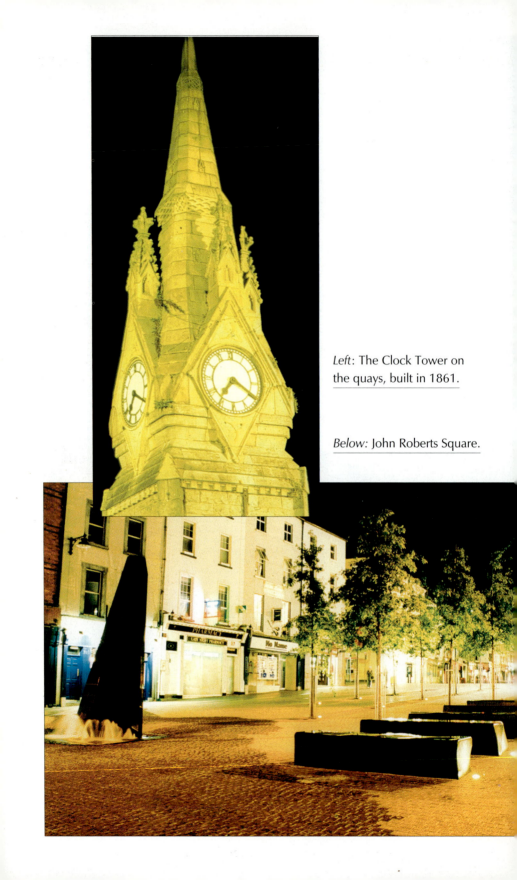

Left: The Clock Tower on the quays, built in 1861.

Below: John Roberts Square.

William Van der Hagen's famous view of Waterford, 1736.

Council Chamber, City Hall, built in 1783.

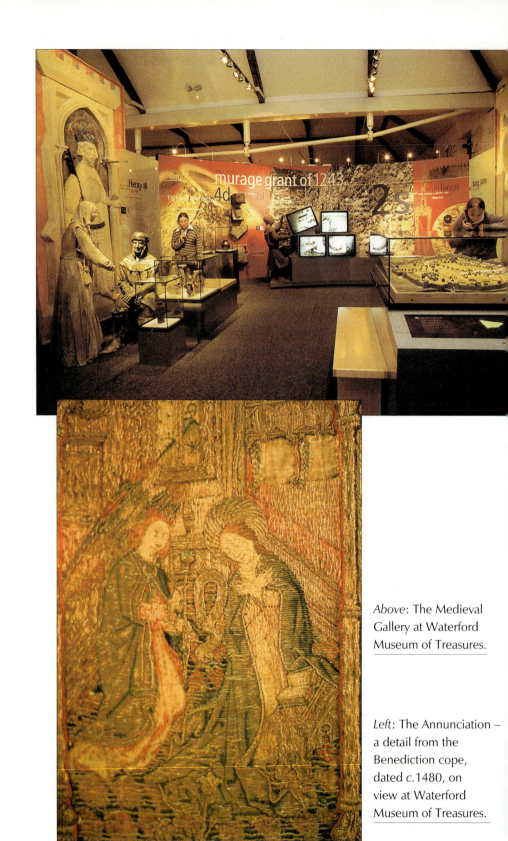

Above: The Medieval Gallery at Waterford Museum of Treasures.

Left: The Annunciation – a detail from the Benediction cope, dated *c.*1480, on view at Waterford Museum of Treasures.

Above: Anglo-Norman ring brooch (*c.*1210), the earliest found in Europe, from Waterford city excavations. Now on view at Waterford Museum of Treasures.

Left: Viking Age kite brooch, *c.*1100, from the Waterford city excavations. Now on view at Waterford Museum of Treasures.

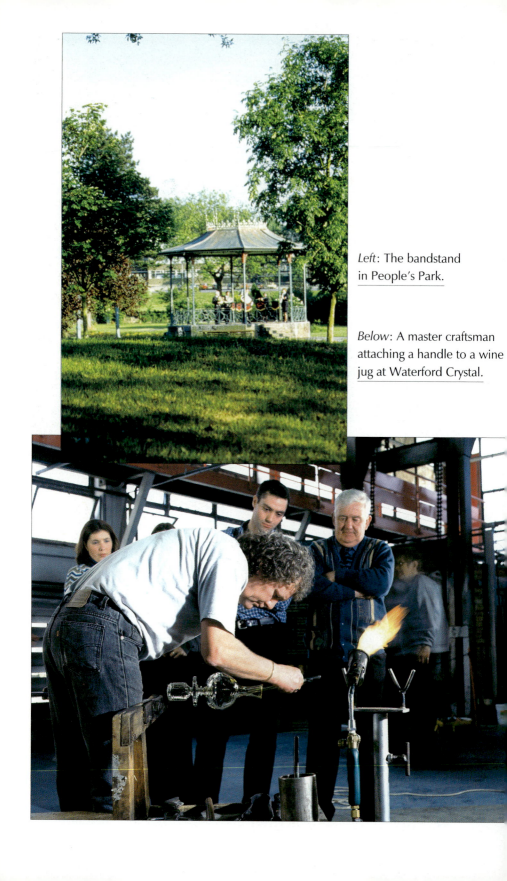

Left: The bandstand in People's Park.

Below: A master craftsman attaching a handle to a wine jug at Waterford Crystal.

The Beach Tower – part of the medieval defences of the city.

Left: Gateway to St Patrick's Church, Jenkin's Lane.

Below: The medieval Franciscan friary, known as Greyfriars, built c.1240.

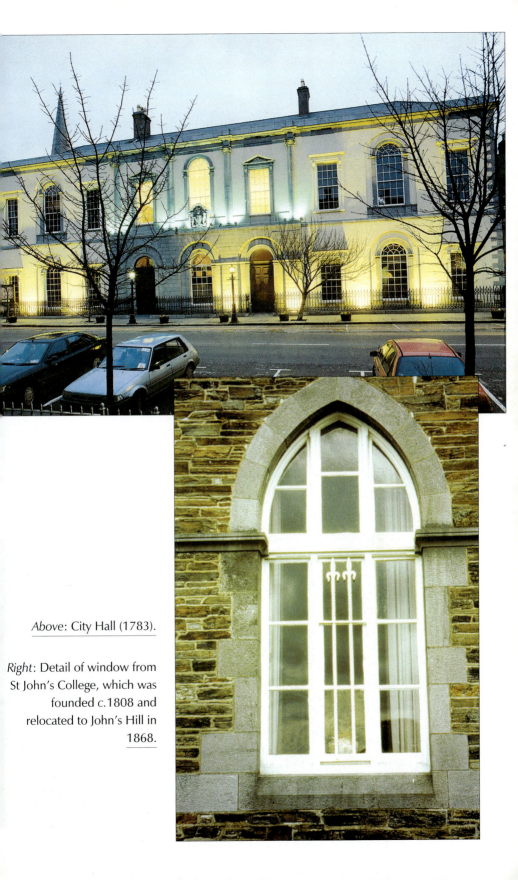

Above: City Hall (1783).

Right: Detail of window from St John's College, which was founded *c.*1808 and relocated to John's Hill in 1868.

Garter Lane Arts Centre, from a performance of *Fire!* from 'Quest'.

Spraoi – the annual August bank holiday street festival and carnival.

Right: The Semi-Lunar Tower, part of the defences of the medieval city.

Below: The millennium sculpture in William Vincent Wallace Plaza, inspired by Viking ships and the marriage of Strongbow and Aoife.

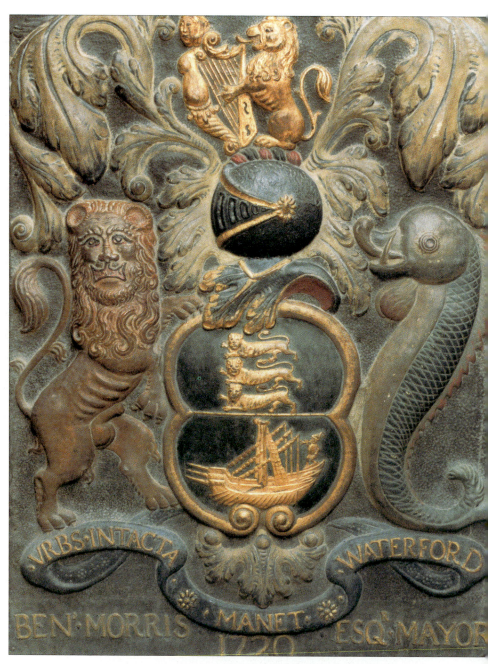

The coat of arms of Waterford, 1720.

GUIDE TO THE HISTORIC CITY

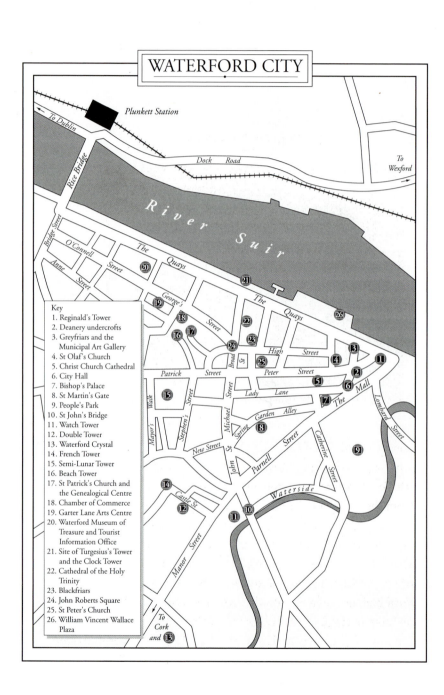

WATERFORD CITY

To Dublin

Plunkett Station

Rice Bridge

Dock   Road

To Wexford

River   Suir

Bridge Street

O'Connell   Street

Anne   Street

The   Quays

George's   Street

The   Quays

Key
1. Reginald's Tower
2. Deanery undercrofts
3. Greyfriars and the Municipal Art Gallery
4. St Olaf's Church
5. Christ Church Cathedral
6. City Hall
7. Bishop's Palace
8. St Martin's Gate
9. People's Park
10. St John's Bridge
11. Watch Tower
12. Double Tower
13. Waterford Crystal
14. French Tower
15. Semi-Lunar Tower
16. Beach Tower
17. St Patrick's Church and the Genealogical Centre
18. Chamber of Commerce
19. Garter Lane Arts Centre
20. Waterford Museum of Treasure and Tourist Information Office
21. Site of Turgesius's Tower and the Clock Tower
22. Cathedral of the Holy Trinity
23. Blackfriars
24. John Roberts Square
25. St Peter's Church
26. William Vincent Wallace Plaza

Patrick   Street

Broad   St

Peter   Street

High   Street

The Mall

Lombard   Street

Mayor's   Walk

Stephen's   Street

Michael   Street

Spring   Garden   Alley

Lady   Lane

Catherine   Street

Castle St

New Street

John   St

Parnell   Street

Waterside

Manor   Street

To Cork and

There are four must-see attractions in Waterford city: (1) Waterford Crystal; (2) Waterford Museum of Treasures; (3) Reginald's Tower and the Viking Triangle – a compact area in the old city where the majority of the medieval and eighteenth-century monuments are located; and (4) the medieval town walls.

WATERFORD CRYSTAL

Waterford Crystal showrooms.

Waterford Crystal, producers of the world's finest cut crystal, is ranked among the top four visitor attractions in Ireland. It is situated about three kilometres from the city centre on the N25, the road that leads from the city to Cork and Kerry. The factory tour is most engaging, introducing the visitor to the whole crystal-making process: blowing, cutting, polishing and engraving. The tour is designed to allow the visitor see the process close-up, almost through the eyes of the artisan, and having completed it, it is easy to understand why Waterford had earned a worldwide reputation for superb craftsmanship. An imaginative audio-visual presentation relives the excitement of the dawn of the new millennium when the Waterford Crystal Millennium Ball descended over Times Square in New York. In the showrooms the full range of crystalware, from chandeliers to salt cellars and from ships' decanters to champagne flutes, is on display, comprising the largest selection of Waterford crystal in the world. A brief history of glass manufacturing in Waterford can be found in the first part of this book, while the guided tour at Waterford Crystal also gives the visitor a historical background to the craft that has made the city famous throughout the world.

WATERFORD MUSEUM OF TREASURES

Waterford Museum of Treasures, which is situated on Merchants' Quay and occupies a converted nineteenth-century granary, is a must for anyone wishing to get a flavour of the history of Ireland's oldest city. The exhibition has won several awards, both for the quality of the exhibits and the way in which the displays bring the historic objects to life in imaginative and unexpected ways. While examining 1,000-year-old Viking Age ships' timbers, you suddenly find yourself in a Viking ship sailing to Waterford in heavy seas – the seats actually sway! As you view the only complete medieval bow in either Ireland or Britain and the actual arrows fired at the city by Strongbow's army in August 1170, you are drawn into a re-enactment of the marriage of Strongbow and Aoife as a witness to this historic event.

The museum is bursting at the seams with unique artefacts, such as the Great Charter Roll, dating from 1215 to 1372, described as late medieval Ireland's answer to the Book of Kells. The four-metre-long roll contains charters, inquisitions and beautifully coloured illustrations of government officials, medieval mayors and some five kings of England. The roll is imaginatively brought to life by an

The old granary building on the quay that houses the
Waterford Museum of Treasures.

The Medieval Gallery at Waterford Museum of Treasures.

interactive display, designed ostensibly for children but also a great attraction for young-at-heart adults.

The Great Parchment Book, begun in 1361 and with the final entry made while Cromwell's army was laying siege outside the gates of the city in 1649, is another object of international importance. It is the earliest recorded use of the English language for official purposes in Ireland. The book is brought to life by an audio-visual presentation that takes a tongue-in-cheek look at some of the medieval legislation contained in it. The Magi Cope, a cope of gold Benediction cloth dating from 1480, is regarded as a great work of medieval art and is part of the only complete set of medieval High Mass vestments to have survived the Reformation in either Britain or Ireland. Henry VIII's cap of maintenance, a gift to the mayor of Waterford in 1536, is the oldest cap of maintenance in western Europe and the only item of that king's clothing to have survived to the present day.

The history of glass-making in the city forms a large part of the eighteenth-century gallery, which houses a fine collection of early Waterford glass, including one of the earliest decanters that has the name Penrose (the family that established the glass-house) impressed on its base. The nineteenth-century gallery features the life and times of Thomas Francis Meagher, the Irish revolutionary leader, hero of the American Civil War and first governor of Montana. In 1848 Meagher brought the first tricolour of green, white and gold to Ireland from Paris, later adopted as the national flag. Part of Meagher's American Civil War uniform, together with his Civil War swords, is also on view. The exhibition ends with an audio-visual presentation, introducing the visitor to the architectural delights of the city in a most imaginative and relaxing programme. The museum is an excellent place to get a comprehensive, easily digested introduction not only to the history of the city but also of Ireland as a whole over the last 1,000 years.

The museum also houses a gift shop and artists' studios. In the studios, visitors are invited to watch silversmiths and artists creating contemporary works of art and can even mint their own silver medieval coins. There is also a restaurant with adjoining courtyard, allowing alfresco dining during the summer months. All age groups are catered for in this building, which is completely accessible to visitors using wheelchairs. The main tourist office for the southeast region is also located in the museum building.

THE VIKING TRIANGLE

Reginald's Tower, situated on the quays, stands at the apex of what is known as the Viking Triangle – the historic quarter of the city. The buildings in the historic city can be conveniently explored by starting from either Reginald's Tower or Waterford Museum of Treasures. The walking distance between the tower and the museum is about ten minutes, however allow at least an hour if you plan to visit all of the important buildings. From March to October entertaining and informative guided walking tours of the historic city are available, commencing at 11.45am and 1.45pm from Waterford Museum of Treasures. The key buildings in the historic city are all numbered on the locator map at the beginning of this section.

REGINALD'S TOWER

Reginald's Tower is the oldest civic urban building in Ireland. The present structure was built on the site of the original Viking fort and named after Regnall, grandson of Ivor the Boneless, who founded the city in AD914. A defensive tower stood on this site during the Viking period and when the city fell to the Anglo-Normans in 1170 it was used as a prison. The tower is the only civic urban monument in Ireland to retain its Norse or Viking name.

Interior of Reginald's Tower.

Both the ground and first floors of the present structure date from 1185 when Henry II's son, Prince John, visited Waterford and ordered the refortification of the old Viking city. The top two floors of the monument were added in either the fifteenth or the sixteenth century to facilitate the use of artillery. Throughout the medieval period the tower was the most important structure on the circuit of stone walls and towers that enclosed and protected the city.

The tower has been in continuous use for over 800 years, and even a cursory look at some of the historic characters and events associated with it will help to explain why it is a must-see attraction on any visit to Waterford. It was here that two of the last Viking rulers of the city were executed in 1170. King Henry II, the first English king to visit Ireland, gave the tower the distinction of being the first English prison in Ireland when he imprisoned the Norman knight Robert Fitz Stephen here in 1171.

A mint was established in the tower by Prince John in 1185, and again in 1210 when John was king of England. In 1399 Richard II, king of England and lord of Ireland, departed Ireland in haste from Waterford harbour, only to find himself deposed on his return home and replaced by Henry Bolingbroke who became Henry IV. In 1463, by order of the Irish parliament, then meeting in Waterford, silver coins emblazoned with the words *Civitas Waterford* were struck here. A few years later, in 1495, cannon fire from this tower sunk one of the ships of the pretender to the English throne, Perkin Warbeck, helping to bring to an end the first artillery siege of an Irish city. After this siege the city received from King Henry VII its motto: *Urbs Intacta Manet* – Waterford remains the untaken city.

In 1570 the English adventurer Thomas Stucley (allegedly the ille-
gitimate son of Henry VIII, and also the man who advised King Philip
II of Spain that by seizing Waterford and stationing a fleet there he
could strangle England's growing power) became involved with the
story of the tower. With the aid of Venetian pirates, he carried off the
bronze cannon that stood on the blockhouse in front of the tower,
protecting the port. A few years later, Stucley was killed while helping the prince of Portugal in a war in northern Africa. In 1650, during
the Cromwellian siege of the city, a cannon ball, which can still be
seen to this day, lodged in the wall of the tower.

In 1690 James II, the last Catholic monarch of England, Scotland
and Ireland, is said to have climbed to the top of the tower to take a
last look at his lost kingdom before sailing to exile in France. In the
eighteenth century the tower escaped destruction when the remaining medieval defensive walls and towers along the quay were pulled
down. In the early nineteenth century it was used as a prison for
'sturdy beggars and debtors', and later in that century it became the
home of the high constable of the city, continuing as a residence
until 1954 when it became a museum.

Reginald's Tower Museum is a very fine, small museum, exhibiting
many original artefacts. The exhibition focuses on both the history of
the building and the development of the city's defences, imaginatively brought to life through a series of models and an absorbing
audio-visual presentation. The second floor is dedicated to the history of the various mints that were housed here from the twelfth to
the fifteenth centuries. Examples of the coins minted in the tower
are on display, including recently recovered archaeological objects
associated with the story of money and coinage in the medieval city.

THE MEDIEVAL UNDERCROFTS

Situated at the top of Bailey's New Street, about a three minute walk
from Reginald's Tower, are the conjoined deanery undercrofts,
cellar-like structures located under the early eighteenth-century
deanery building (now the offices of Waterford Corporation). The
earliest undercroft dates from the thirteenth century and was probably built as a mint by Stephen Fulbourne, governor of Ireland and
bishop of Waterford, in about 1281. The upper floors of what, in

medieval times, was a substantial deanery were removed many centuries ago, but the survival of this elaborate, stone-built undercroft remains unique in Irish urban archaeology. Archaeological excavations of the floor of the undercroft revealed the foundation of a substantial stone building that predated the Anglo-Norman invasion of 1170, suggesting that a deanery or other important building stood on this site during the late Viking Age.

The fifteenth-century upper undercroft at the Deanery, Cathedral Square.

Bishop Stephen Fulbourne probably commissioned the building as a mint. In the 1280s he was governor of Ireland, and therefore the most important man in the country at that time. This double-jobbing was not unusual during the medieval period as monarchs often elevated royal officials, many of whom were educated clergymen, to vacant bishoprics. A bishopric usually carried with it a large estate, and the rents from these lands would have provided a generous income for the fortunate official. (It is interesting to note that because most of the royal bookkeepers were drawn from the ranks of the educated clergy and known as clerks (from the Latin *clericus*), we still refer to bookkeepers as clerks.) When Fulbourne was relieved of his post as governor of Ireland, he was compensated by the king who elevated him to the position of archbishop of Tuam. His removal from office had a big impact on Waterford because his replacement had Cork associations and the mint was transferred for a short time to that city. Coins from Fulbourne's mint are on display at Reginald's Tower Museum, and at Waterford Museum of Treasures visitors can strike their own exact silver replicas of these coins.

The thirteenth-century lower undercroft at the Deanery, Cathedral Square.

A series of steps lead from Stephen Fulbourne's thirteenth-century undercroft to what is called the upper undercroft. More basic in its construction – it does not feature the cut-stone pillars or door mouldings of the lower undercroft – it nonetheless boasts an almost perfect example of wicker-centring in its stone roof. This undercroft dates from the early fifteenth century and belonged to medieval Waterford's most famous mayor, James Rice, whose macabre cadaver tomb can be seen in the nearby Church of Ireland Cathedral. We know from the Register of the Chantry of St Saviour's, kept by dean John Collyn, that this undercroft was given by James Rice to the dean on 6 July 1468. The register records property given to the dean for the upkeep of an almshouse, known as the Good Mens' House. The existence of such an institution in late fifteenth-century Waterford suggests a high level of prosperity in the city. After it was acquired, the undercroft and the building above it were incorporated into the deanery complex. The door of the undercroft faces the quay where its former owner, James Rice, has his own private dock. We can safely presume that the undercroft was used as a store, possibly for wine; surviving records note that Rice had extensive trading links with Spain.

THE FRENCH CHURCH

A minute's walk from the undercrofts is the substantial ruin of the city's thirteenth-century Franciscan friary, also known as the French

Church, built about 1240 – only fourteen years after the death of St Francis of Assisi, the founder of the order. According to tradition the building was financed by Sir Hugh Purcell, an Anglo-Norman knight.

The friars were known for their generosity and usually ministered to the poor of the city. They were much loved by the citizens and during the medieval period a number of monks buried in the associated graveyard were venerated as saints. During the thirteenth century the friars received an annual allowance for the purchase of new habits from Henry III of England. Their habits were made from undyed grey woollen cloth, the cheapest available, and worn as a sign of humility. It was from the colour of their habits that they became known as greyfriars, and today the street in which the friary stands is still called Greyfriars Street. In 1394 Richard II lodged here while making plans for his assault on the Gaelic Irish in the Wicklow Mountains, and we know that it was here he received the submissions of Turloch O'Connor Don of Connaught, and other notable Irish chieftains and princes.

The French Church, Greyfriars.

A bell tower almost twenty-five metres high with a typically Irish parapet and stepped battlements was added to the friary in the late fifteenth century. The friary was dissolved by order of Henry VIII in 1540, and in 1544 Henry Walsh, a wealthy Waterford merchant, received a charter from Henry VIII to convert it into an almshouse, which was known as the Hospital of the Holy Ghost. The Walshs were driven from the city during the Cromwellian period. They took up residence in the Canary Islands and became involved in the wine business. Yet despite religious differences, for many years the Protestant corporation that now controlled the city allowed the exiled Walshs to appoint Catholic masters to the hospital each time the post became vacant. The hospital or almshouse remained on this site until 1815 when it transferred to the suburbs. Still in operation today, it is one of the oldest charitable institutions in Ireland.

During the Reformation, statues from various churches in the city were brought to the almshouse for safe-keeping. They comprise the largest set of medieval statues in Ireland and are now on display in Waterford Museum of Treasures. In 1542 the great garden and quay of the friary were given by the corporation to David Bailey, a local merchant, and he subsequently laid out Bailey's New Street, connecting the present friary to Reginald's Tower.

In 1693, under the patronage of William of Orange, King William III of England, the corporation encouraged French Huguenots to settle in Waterford and establish a linen industry. The Protestant bishop Nathaniel Foy had the choir of the old friary fitted out for their religious service, hence the name the French Church. The Catholic almshouse and the Huguenot house of worship coexisted peacefully on this site for over a century. Tradition credits the Huguenots with introducing the now famous Waterford blaa, a very popular and delicious breakfast bread found only in Waterford city. The French called it *pain blanc,* which was corrupted by Waterfordians to blaa. It is a delicacy that should not be missed by visitors to Waterford and is pined after by Waterfordians in exile.

Among the distinguished persons buried in the friary is Sir Niall O'Neill of County Antrim, who fought for King James II at the Battle of the Boyne and who was wounded while defending the ford at Rossnaree. He was taken to Waterford where he died shortly afterwards at the early age of thirty-two. O'Neill's monument now stands against the wall on the left-hand side of the chancel. Beneath the tower arch lies the unadorned limestone graveslab of the city's most famous architect, John Roberts.

THE MUNICIPAL ART GALLERY

View of Waterford by John Roberts's son, Thomas Sautelle Roberts, 1795.

Next to the French Church is the former Methodist Church, which opened as the Municipal Art Gallery in 2001 following refurbishment by Waterford Corporation. The gallery displays part of the extensive municipal collection of contemporary Irish art, and also hosts visiting exhibitions. Almost every important twentieth-century artist is featured in the collection, including Jack B Yeats, Louis Le Brocquy and Paul Henry.

CHRIST CHURCH CATHEDRAL

About two minutes' walk from the Municipal Gallery and French Church is the Cathedral of the Most Holy Trinity, Christ Church. This very fine neo-classical Church of Ireland (Protestant) cathedral was built during the 1770s and is the work of the Waterford-born architect John Roberts (1714–1796). It replaced a Gothic cathedral built on this site in 1210 and demolished in 1773. The cathedral has been described by Mark Girouard, a noted architectural historian, as the finest eighteenth-century ecclesiastical building in Ireland. He describes the spire as:

... particularly satisfying, built in the same cool grey limestone as the Bishop's Palace, and soars up from its square base to its octagonal steeple in a series of delicately modulating stages. St Martin-in-the-Fields, London, and other spires by John Gibbs are obvious sources of inspiration, but the Waterford spire is not a copy but an original creation.

Roberts was the builder as well as the architect of the cathedral. Inside, the plan is unusual in that it has an open ante-chapel, probably originally intended as a baptistery at the west end, similar to the college chapels of Oxford and Cambridge. A number of monuments from the old cathedral were erected in this ante-chapel, including the 1482 tomb of James Rice; a series of glass panels on the wall behind the tomb tells the story of his unusual life. Here also

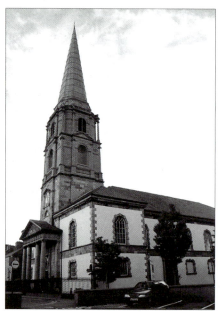

Christ Church Cathedral.

part of the floor has been removed to reveal a portion of a pillar from the Gothic, early thirteenth-century cathedral. A series of glass panels gives a brief history of the cathedral since its foundation in 1096.

The cathedral has had an eventful history. It is the seat of the second oldest bishopric on the island. It was here that the Anglo-Norman lord Strongbow married Aoife, an Irish princess, a union which changed the course of Irish history. King John endowed the cathedral in about 1210 and soon after work began on the building of a new Gothic structure. That cathedral, along with Christ Church Cathedral and St Patrick's Cathedral in Dublin, was regarded as one of the finest medieval cathedrals in Ireland. During the early thirteenth century it was rife with intrigue as the bishops of Waterford attempted to annex the neighbouring diocese of Lismore. In 1203 Pope Innocent III had even excommunicated bishop Robert of Waterford (Anglo-Norman) in an attempt to prevent the hostile take-over bid by Waterford. Robert's successor, Bishop David, pursued the annexation until he was killed by an Irishman, probably a supporter of the (Gaelic Irish) bishop of Lismore. The Waterford bishops persisted and after almost two centuries of agitation succeeded in uniting the two dioceses. When King Richard II made his first visit to Waterford in 1394 he witnessed the installation of the first bishop of the united dioceses of Waterford and Lismore. The bishop, Robert Reed (an Englishman), had been appointed a month before Richard sailed for Ireland. Bishop Reed is said to have intoned the *Te Deum* as the royal party entered the cathedral for his first public Mass in Waterford. During the late fifteenth century a number of side chapels were added, the most well-known being that of James Rice in 1482, built in nine months and consecrated by an outsider, the bishop of Ossory (Kilkenny), because James Rice and the dean of the cathedral, John Collyn, refused to accept or admit to the cathedral the recently appointed bishop of Waterford and Lismore on the grounds that he could not speak English.

During the reign of Queen Elizabeth the cathedral became the property of the Church of Ireland. When the city fell to Cromwellian forces in 1650 the cathedral was looted and William Bolton, a Cromwellian captain, attired in jackboots, preached a fiery sermon from the pulpit. When it came to demolishing the Gothic cathedral in 1773 to make way for the present structure, explosives had to be used because it had been built so well. One positive outcome of the demolition was the discovery of the now famous Waterford vestments. Dating from the late medieval period they are the only complete set of either British or Irish High Mass vestments to survive the Reformation. On discovery of the vestments the Church of Ireland bishop presented them to the Roman Catholic dean of Waterford. They were placed on loan in the National Museum of Ireland, Dublin, in the 1950s for safe-keeping. One of the set, a magnificent Benediction cope of gold Italian cloth dating from 1480, has been fully conserved by Waterford Corporation with the help of a grant from the Heritage Council and is on display at Waterford Museum of Treasures. The loss of the city's medieval cathedral was indeed a great tragedy. However, the citizens may be consoled by the fact that John Roberts's liking for the lightness and elegance of the classical style ensured that in Christ Church Cathedral, Waterford has today the finest eighteenth-century ecclesiastical building in Ireland.

THE BISHOP'S PALACE

A minute's walk from the cathedral is the Bishop's Palace; the rear of the palace actually faces the south side of the cathedral. The palace has been described by Dr Peter Galloway as one of the largest and finest Episcopal residences in Ireland. Now housing the engineering department of Waterford Corporation, the palace was begun in the early 1740s. Mark Girouard describes it as being 'built of beautifully cut limestone ashlar and has the handsome reticence of the best Irish Georgian architecture'. It was designed by Richard Castle, the German architect whose work in Ireland includes Powerscourt House, Russborough House, Westport House and Carton House, and in Dublin the seat of Dáil Éireann, Leinster House. The front of the palace faces on to the Mall, created only a few years prior to the construction of the palace when the Pill or St John's River was diverted and the area it had occupied was drained. The thirteenth-century town wall that ran along the edge of the property was incorporated into the formal stepped gardens that were a feature of the palace.

The Bishop's Palace, now the engineering department
of Waterford Corporation.

Bishop Charles Este, who was born in Whitehall, London in 1696, was responsible for commissioning the palace. Educated at Oxford, he brought a cosmopolitan style to the city and even sat for the famous Anglo-French portrait painter Jean Baptiste van Loo, whose subjects included the king and queen of France. A man of taste and culture, it is not surprising that he should commission the most renowned architect of the period to design the palace. Este had a very clear view of the type of palace he required, and in a letter sent to the archbishop of Cashel he sought approval to demolish the old palace and build the new, outlining in detail his requirements. Today the interior finishes correspond to those detailed in Este's letter to the archbishop. Bishop Este died in 1745, leaving the palace unfinished; his successor, Bishop Chenevix, employed John Roberts to oversee the completion of the building. A portrait of Charles Este, a short-lived bishop, aged only forty-nine years when he died, hangs in Waterford Museum of Treasures.

Charles Este, bishop of Waterford (1696–1745), attributed to Jean Baptiste van Loo (1684–1745).

FROM THE BISHOP'S PALACE TO CITY HALL

As you stand at the front door of the Bishop's Palace, instead of walking down the main steps in front of the palace, turn left and you will come to a series of limestone steps. Follow the steps down until you exit at a lower level. Now you are at the entrance to the Theatre Royal, part of the eighteenth-century City Hall building. This area is particularly interesting. The limestone steps that bring you from the upper level of the Bishop's Garden down to the lower level are built in the remains of a seventeenth- or eighteenth-century cellar, which itself is built against a portion of the thirteenth-century town wall. The town wall actually runs in front of the palace and behind City Hall. When this area was archaeologically excavated, an early quay wall, which ran parallel to the town wall, was discovered, and beneath it what appears to be a floor timber from a Viking Age ship was unearthed. The discovery was not completely unexpected as this is the site of the tidal inlet where Regnall and his band of invading Vikings first moored their longboats and created a permanent *longphort* settlement.

CITY HALL

City Hall was designed by John Roberts and work began on the building in 1783, the same year the Penrose family established their glass-house. In that year the chief merchants of the city acquired the lease of the land where City Hall now stands for the purpose of erecting a playhouse and assembly rooms, and it was agreed that the mayor of the city was to have full use of the entire ground floor for public entertainment. In 1813 the corporation bought out the remainder of the lease and moved the city offices from the Exchange on the quay to City Hall, where they remain to this day. The Large Room, known in the eighteenth century as the Grand Banqueting Room, has welcomed such notable figures as Daniel O'Connell, Thomas Francis Meagher, Isaac Butt, Charles Stewart Parnell and John Redmond. King Edward VII was also received here in 1904. In 1916 it was to be the venue for the annual fête, but that had to be cancelled when the Easter Rising broke out. The following year a *ceilí mór* (great dance) did go ahead, and among those present were Seán T Ó Ceallaigh and Eamon de Valera, both later to become presidents of Ireland and Honorary Freemen of Waterford. In 1994 president Mary Robinson, later UN High Commissioner for Human Rights, was conferred with the Honorary Freedom of the City here.

The Council Chamber, City Hall.

In the adjoining council chamber hangs William Van der Hagen's famous view of Waterford, the earliest view of an Irish city. The painting was commissioned in 1736 by the corporation for the princely sum of £20. The central chandelier in the chamber, dating from the mid-1780s, is the largest and oldest piece of Waterford glass extant, and was originally commissioned for the Presence Chamber in Dublin Castle, where it hung until 1836. It is interesting to note that the architect of the Presence Chamber was Thomas Penrose, cousin of the owner of the newly opened Waterford Glass Factory. In order to secure the order for his cousin, Thomas Penrose persuaded the lord lieutenant of Ireland, the duke of Rutland, to visit Waterford and view the work of the glass-house; it was during this visit that the order was placed. Council meetings are held in this chamber twice monthly, chaired by the mayor who is elected annually.

City Hall also houses the office of the city manager and the Mayor's Parlour, where for nearly 200 years the mayor has entertained visiting dignitaries. In the foyer is a series of plaques erected in 1995 to celebrate 800 years of civic government in Waterford. The names of over 600 mayors are listed, and each year the outgoing mayor adds his name to the plaque.

THE THEATRE ROYAL

City Hall also houses the Band Room, as it was known in the eighteenth century. In 1876 this room was remodelled to create a beautiful, Victorian, horseshoe-shaped theatre. The theatre is small and intimate, seating about 600 people, and is much loved by the theatre-going and music-loving population of the city. Each year since 1947 the theatre has hosted the Waterford International Festival of Light Opera. The city's love affair with music and theatre can be traced back many centuries, however it was in the nineteenth century that Waterford produced its most notable actor, Charles Kean, and its most notable composer, William Vincent Wallace.

A plaque on a house at the top of Colbeck Street (the street running to the south of the Bishop's Palace) tells us that these two great

Charles Kean as Hamlet.

nineteenth-century figures were actually born in the same house. Charles Kean was born in 1811 and he went on to become a renowned Shakespearean actor, performing in London, Edinburgh and New York, where he appeared at the Park Theatre as Richard III. A member of the Covent Garden Company in London, he became a very wealthy man from his acting career. In 1837, on hearing that the New Theatre Royal in Bolton Street, Waterford, had been destroyed by fire, Kean wrote to the owner and offered his services free of charge and 'to play in a barn if necessary' in order to raise funds to rebuild it. An equally successful figure in the field of music, William Vincent Wallace, one of Ireland's best-known composers, was born in 1812. A bronze bust of him by Seamus Murphy RHA adorns the garden of the Bishop's Palace. The new plaza on the quay, built as the city's millennium project, was dedicated to Wallace's memory in 2001.

ST OLAF'S CHURCH

As you leave City Hall, turn right and walk along the Mall in front of the Bishop's Palace where you will see two nineteenth-century cannons that were captured by the British Army following the Battle of Sebastopol in 1854 during the Crimean War. At the next junction,

St Olaf's Church.

walk up Colbeck Street and past the house where Kean and Wallace were born. Take a left turn into Lady Lane and then take an immediate right turn into Saint Francis Place, passing the rear of the Widows' Apartments, built in 1702 by Hugh Gore for the widows of Church of Ireland clergymen; today it houses widows and widowers of all denominations.

Here in Francis Street you will find the Franciscan Church, opened in 1834. It is designed with impressive classical simplicity, based on a monumental Ionic order. At the end of this street stands the Church of St Olaf, built by Bishop Thomas Milles in 1734 – a building of few architectural pretensions. Milles, though a learned man, was regarded with suspicion by his ultra-Protestant flock. Dean Jonathan Swift, the famous Dublin author of *Gulliver's Travels,* reported that Milles was suspected by his brethren of wearing a crucifix. Both the dedication to St Olaf, a Norwegian saint, and its location in the centre of the old Viking city suggest that the church was originally a Viking foundation. It was also rebuilt in the Anglo-Norman period and part of the medieval gable, still visible, is incorporated into the eighteenth-century rebuilding.

ST PETER'S CHURCH

From St Olaf's Church, walk into City Square Shopping Centre and take the escalator that leads down to the underground car park. At the end of the escalator you will see, housed behind a wall of glass, the foundations of the twelfth-century St Peter's Church, one of the oldest parish churches in the city.

Viking Age burial from the archaeologically excavated St Peter's graveyard.

St Peter's was excavated by Waterford Corporation during the major archaeological examination of the site that took place between 1986 and 1992, when over 6,000 square metres were archaeologically resolved prior to the current development. The foundations show that the church had a semicircular apse – a unique feature in twelfth-century Irish ecclesiastical architecture. Its dedication to St Peter, the apostle and first pope, could well reflect the triumph of the Roman Reform Movement in Irish Church affairs following the Council of Cashel in AD1101. The many thousands of objects recovered from this site are now stored at Waterford Museum of Treasures, where the more important objects from the excavation, such as Viking Age and Anglo-Norman jewellery, form part of the permanent exhibition.

BLACKFRIARS

On leaving City Square Shopping Centre, take the High Street exit and as you leave the building you will see the tower of Blackfriars. If you walk down Conduit Lane to your right, you will have a better view of the ruins of this mid-thirteenth-century friary, known as St Saviour's or Blackfriars. The friary is also known as Blackfriars because the Dominican order who occupied the friary wore black habits. In time it became traditional for all academics to wear black, and so the black gown worn by academics today owes its origins to the black habits of the thirteenth-century Dominicans.

The Dominicans who built the friary at Blackfriars first settled in Waterford in 1226. The site for their building was a gift from the citizens of Waterford, who had to seek permission from Henry III before they could make the grant. Interestingly, the petitioners described the site as a void area within the walls of their city, where, in ancient times, an old tower had once stood. We know from a document dated 1311 that one of the leaders of the Ostmen or Vikings, Gerald Macgillemory, lived in this tower at the time of the Anglo-Norman invasion. The same Gerald, because of the assistance he gave the Anglo-Normans at the time of the invasion, was

Ruins of the thirteenth-century Blackfriars with its late fifteenth-century bell tower.

given special privileges by Henry II upon his arrival in Waterford in 1171.

A plaque on the wall of the friary records the fact that one of the monks who lived here was Geoffrey of Waterford. A scholar of Greek, Arabic and Latin and highly regarded as a wine expert, Geoffrey died in Paris in about 1300. The friary's bell tower, like that of Greyfriars or the French Church, was built in the late fifteenth century. In 1916 the clapper of a bell from this tower was found partially buried here. And in 2000, a short distance away, a large bronze bell, believed to be from the bell tower, was unearthed. Also like Greyfriars, Blackfriars was dissolved in 1540 by order of King Henry VIII. The friary was subsequently used as a courthouse from 1617, and was used as a theatre in 1746.

The Dominicans were an important asset to the city. They were an intellectual order who organised schools and educated the sons of the merchant class. They were also a preaching order and often gave public sermons at a stone canopy-adorned cross that once stood at the east end of Patrick Street. Though this structure has long since vanished, the area is still referred to locally as The Cross.

JOHN ROBERTS SQUARE

From Blackfriars, return to High Street and walking via Blackfriars Lane make your way to John Roberts Square. This area, lying immediately outside the old Viking town, was developed during the Anglo-Norman expansion of the thirteenth century. It was pedestrianised in 2000, and dedicated to the memory of John Roberts, the Waterford-born, eighteenth-century architect and builder.

John Roberts (1714–1796) was the grandson of Thomas Roberts, 'a Welshman of property' who settled in Waterford about 1680; his father was a builder. At the age of about seventeen, John eloped with Mary Susannah Sautelle, daughter of a Waterford Huguenot family. They were forced to elope because Roberts's family felt that Mary was beneath his station as she came from a poorer family. The marriage worked out well – they had twenty-two children, although only eight survived to adulthood. Richard Chenevix, the bishop of Waterford, was also of Huguenot stock and a friend of the Sautelles, so he employed John to finish the works on the new Bishop's Palace, which had been started by bishop Este in the early 1740s. Chenevix also gave the young couple a lease on the old Bishop's Palace, which stood on the top of Cathedral Square, and this became their home.

In January 1774 the cathedral committee selected Roberts's plan for the new Christ Church Cathedral; no doubt the bishop's support helped to sway the decision. Roberts was also responsible for the building of City Hall, both the Catholic and Protestant cathedrals, the Morris family home in George's Street (now the Chamber of Commerce building), the County and City Infirmary, Newtown School (the former home of John Wyse) and some miles from the city, near Portlaw, County Waterford, the forecourt of Curraghmore House, home of lord Waterford.

John Roberts Square.

Curraghmore and its surrounding landscape became the subject of a watercolour by Thomas Sautelle Roberts, John's son. Thomas Sautelle was an important nineteenth-century painter and founder member of the Royal Hibernian Academy (RHA). Indeed, John's great-grandson was the equally famous field-marshal earl Roberts (1832–1914), commander-in-chief of British forces in Ireland from 1895 to 1899. A clock presented to earl Roberts stands in the foyer of the Granville Hotel on the quay.

However, it was John Roberts the architect who left the most enduring impression on the city of his birth. As an architect, he stands tall among his eighteenth-century peers. As a builder, he was at the very least remarkable and was known in his day as Honest John Roberts. It is to his lasting credit that he was asked to build both cathedrals in his home city. He had the intellect and integrity to respect both liturgical traditions, and as a result he gave the two buildings absolutely different characters, each suited to its own philosophy. To quote Mark Girouard:

... the Protestant Cathedral is cool and northern, redo-
lent of lawn sleeves and communion service; the
Catholic Cathedral, with its forest of huge Corinthian
columns, is warm, luscious and Mediterranean.

THE CATHEDRAL CHURCH OF THE MOST HOLY TRINITY

From John Roberts Square walk towards the Clock Tower on the quay
and you will find, set back from the main line of buildings, the
impressive façade of the Catholic cathedral with its Ionic stone front
facing on to the street. The cathedral is built on the site of a former
Catholic chapel that the Roman Catholic community petitioned the
corporation to build in 1700. This was an undistinguished building,
concealed from public gaze by housing that fronted onto Barronstrand Street. The entry to the chapel at this time was from Conduit
Lane by a long narrow passage.

The present cathedral, built between 1793 and 1796, is the oldest
Roman Catholic cathedral in either Britain or Ireland (all the ancient
Roman Catholic cathedrals became the property of the Church of
Ireland during the Reformation). Roberts was over eighty years old

Cathedral Church of the Most Holy Trinity, Barronstrand Street, c.1895.

when he designed it. His custom was to rise at 6am each morning to superintend the workmen. One morning he rose at 3am by mistake and found the cathedral empty. He sat down, fell asleep and caught a chill from which he died. The classical cathedral that he left almost complete is basically a rectangle with an apsidal east end. Shallow four-bay recesses on the north and south sides may be taken as the architectural descendants of transepts. Today, eight large crystal chandeliers – a gift from Waterford Crystal – light the interior, which has a dark and sultry atmosphere. However, there is no feeling of oppressiveness, only a welcome refuge from the crowded clamour of the city outside.

The façade of the Roman Catholic cathedral roughly marks the western limit of the Viking Triangle, but in the Anglo-Norman suburbs there is a number of very interesting buildings, three of which are *en route* from John Roberts Square to Waterford Museum of Treasures.

From John Roberts Square, walk into George's Street and look out for a small lane to your left where you will find both St Patrick's Church and the Genealogical Centre.

ST PATRICK'S CHURCH

St Patrick's Church in Chapel Lane is that great rarity in Ireland: an eighteenth-century Catholic chapel. There are records of Mass being celebrated here as early as 1704. From the outside the building looks like a large storehouse, and tradition holds that during the period when the most oppressive of Penal Laws were enforced against

Catholics, the cornstore on that site was converted for use as a church.

St Patrick's Church.

The church is marked as New Chappel on a 1764 map of Waterford, though access to it at that time was via a much narrower lane
further down George's Street. The interior is a single cell with a
horseshoe-shaped gallery. Like St Olaf's, it is a building with few
architectural pretensions but has considerable charm and is vividly
evocative of the period in which it was built. The church is one of
those hidden gems that will reward those that take the time to find it.

There is also a Church of Ireland St Patrick's Church in the city,
located in Patrick Street, about a four minute walk from its Catholic
counterpart. Built in 1727, it occupies the site of a medieval church,
which was also dedicated to St Patrick. The dedication and its location on the perimeter of the medieval suburbs suggest that the
medieval church served as the place of worship for the inhabitants of
the Irishtown outside the gates of the city. The simple, single-cell,
eighteenth-century, stone-built church that now occupies the site is
plain, like many of the churches from this period, yet has its own
integrity. Today it is a place of worship for members of the Presbyte-
rian–Methodist United Church.

THE GENEALOGICAL CENTRE

The Genealogical Centre, situated at the top of Chapel Lane, is part
of the St Patrick's Church complex and in former times functioned as
the Jesuit house. Here the baptismal, marriage and death records of
the various religious denominations of the dioceses of Waterford and
Lismore are housed, together with census of population records. The
records date back as far as the late eighteenth century. (For a reasonable fee the staff at the centre will carry out commissioned
research.) It was in this building, in 1798, that the Presentation
order of nuns first established themselves in Waterford.

THE BEACH TOWER

From the top of Chapel Lane you can see the Beach Tower with its
typical fifteenth-century Irish crenellations – one of the finest towers
on the circuit of the walls. It was built on a rocky outcrop that forms a
natural defensive position. During the medieval period the area

between the tower and the river was not developed and the tower commanded a fine view of the River Suir and, in particular, of the upriver approaches.

THE CHAMBER OF COMMERCE BUILDING

Chamber of Commerce building.

From the Beach Tower walk, through the car park to George's Street. When you arrive at George's Street the third building/door on your left with the double flight of steps is the Chamber of Commerce building. It was built by John Roberts in the 1780s as the town house of a wealthy Waterford merchant, William Morris. The Morris family were Cromwellian adventurers who settled in the city after 1650 and acquired a substantial stone-built house on the corner of Exchange Street and the quay, next to the Great Quay Gate; the town wall running along the quay acted as the north-facing wall of the house. The house was given a new façade at the beginning of the eighteenth century when the town wall was demolished after advances in artillery had made it redundant, however the sixteenth- or seventeenth-century house remained behind this new façade. Today a large element of this early house is incorporated into the present building, now the Anglo-Irish Bank, an interesting coincidence as in the seventeenth century the building did function for a time as a money exchange. In 1655, following the Cromwellian settlement, John Morris, an ancestor of William Morris, is recorded as having been one of the persons responsible for shipping dispossessed, destitute Catholics to Barbados as indentured servants to the British colonists there.

After William Morris's death in 1815 the house was sold to the Waterford Chamber of Commerce, which had been founded in 1796 and is therefore one of the oldest chambers in Britain or Ireland. The primary objective of the Chamber of Commerce was to promote trade and commerce in the city, which it does very successfully to this day.

The Chamber of Commerce building faces down Gladstone Street and the sheer size of its façade is extremely impressive. The windows of this eighteenth-century town house, as else-

Detail of fine plasterwork in the Chamber of Commerce.

where in Waterford, have been given Victorian surroundings, but the beautiful doorway at the head of the double flight of steps is original and leads to a series of rooms that still retain their exquisite eighteenth-century plasterwork. According to Mark Girouard, the finest feature is 'the oval staircase, one of the most elegant in Ireland. It remains a never-failing delight to walk towards this staircase, follow up the delicate curve of the baluster, and suddenly see the walls blossom out into eagles, swags and garlands high up over one's head.'

GARTER LANE ARTS CENTRE

From the Chamber of Commerce building, continue down O'Connell Street for about thirty metres until you come to an eighteenth-century archway that provides access to a lane leading to Garter Lane Arts Centre. The centre is housed in a Quaker meeting house that was built in 1792, about a year before the Catholic community built their new cathedral.

A performance at Garter Lane Arts Centre, formerly the Quaker meeting house.

Approached through an inconspicuous archway, the entrance gives no idea at all of the size of the eighteenth-century building behind. Its size provides ample testimony to the size and wealth of the eighteenth-century Quaker community in Waterford. It was in this newly developed area outside the old medieval city, and in streets like King Street (now called O'Connell Street after The Liberator) and Hanover Street, where most of the Quaker merchants of Waterford had their homes and business premises. Names like Penrose and Gatchell, both of glass-making fame, Jacob, of biscuit fame – it was in Waterford that Jacob produced the first cream cracker as ships' biscuits, and White, the ship-builders were all to be found here. In total the Quakers made up about two percent of the city's population, but their contribution to the city's economy was tremendous and far outweighed their small number. Streets in this Quaker quarter still echo their presence and their *métiers*: Glasshouse Lane, Penrose Lane, Dyehouse Lane. (Today Dyehouse Lane is the home of a most interesting art gallery and pottery works operated by the renowned Waterford potter Liz McCay.) Despite the great heritage of the Quakers, they are best remembered for their unconditional assistance to the poor and starving who flocked to the city at the time of the Great Famine in the late 1840s. Many members of the Quaker community both financed and operated the soup kitchens that provided life-saving sustenance for the many starving people who arrived in the city.

The meeting house itself contains a large meeting hall, now converted to a beautiful 200-seat theatre in the round, and some smaller rooms. These are separated from the meeting room by a plain entrance foyer, which contains a double-return stairs to the first floor. The severe simplicity of the detail and the plainness of the entire design accords with Quaker tastes; it has much in common with the Shaker tradition of simple, unadorned design, which developed in North America. The entrance yard of the meeting house contains an interesting, untitled concrete casting by Waterford artist and sculptor Joan Walsh-Smith, who has gained a huge reputation all over the Far East, along with her husband Charles, from their current base in Perth, Western Australia.

The meeting house building, now called Garter Lane Arts Centre, is in many ways the centre of artistic and cultural life in Waterford. The acquisition of the building by Waterford Corporation and its conversion, two centuries after being built, to an arts centre has had a tremendous spin-off in theatre, dance, music, youth drama and a vibrant visual arts programme for the city. The city's professional theatre company, Red Kettle, is based and regularly performs here. A lively year-round programme of performances and exhibitions continues the idea and function of the building as a meeting place. The present name, Garter Lane, is a survivor from one of the narrow lanes on the site of the present-day John Roberts Square, removed by the Wide Streets Commission during the mid-nineteenth century.

Moving from Garter Lane further down O'Connell Street, you come to a junction that returns you to the pedestrianised Hanover Street and Waterford Museum of Treasures.

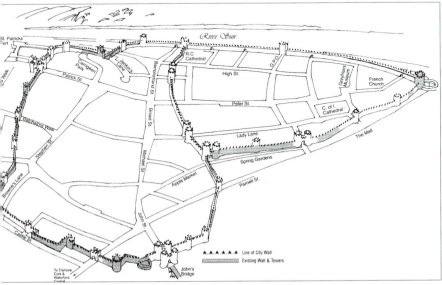

Map showing the town walls of Waterford.

THE TOWN WALLS AND TOWERS
OF MEDIEVAL WATERFORD

With six towers and long stretches of town wall, Waterford boasts the largest collection of medieval defensive towers and walls in Ireland. The best place to start exploring these monuments is at Reginald's Tower, where you will find a series of models that trace the evolution of the defences from the Viking period up to the seventeenth century. Three separate audio-visual presentations explain how the walls were built and how they evolved in response to developments in weaponry (see Reginald's Tower). A series of green plaques will help you locate the towers described below as you follow the circuit from Reginald's Tower. The first plaque is outside the Reginald Bar, to the rear of the tower.

FROM REGINALD'S TOWER TO ST MARTIN'S GATE

Moving on from Reginald's Tower, the town wall ran south through what is today the Reginald Bar; part of the late twelfth-century wall is today incorporated into the pub. From here the wall runs behind City Hall and can be picked up again on the Mall as it passes in front of the Bishop's Palace. Where it crossed Colbeck Street a plaque on a building here marks where Colbeck or St Catherine's Gate once stood. From here the wall runs up Spring Garden Alley. Along this alleyway sections of the thirteenth-century wall can be seen forming the boundary between properties.

The wall terminates at the archaeologically excavated base of St Martin's Gate, a typical thirteenth-century gate and portcullis flanked by twin towers. You can see from what little remains of the gate that the passage or entrance was kept narrow to hinder invaders and to facilitate the collection of the murage, that is, the tax levied on goods brought into the city; the narrow entranceway ensured that only one wagon could pass through at a time. In the later Middle Ages when the gate had become redundant it was greatly altered to facilitate its conversion into a residence known as St Martin's Castle; we do not know who lived in this residence.

During the reign of King John (1199–1215), St Martin's Gate marked the point at which the southern defences ended and took a

right turn to follow north to the River Suir, where the wall terminated at what was called Turgesius's Tower, close to the present-day
Clock Tower. From this point at Turgesius's Tower the wall ran along
the quay to join up again with Reginald's Tower, enclosing a triangular area as it did so. This late twelfth- and early thirteenth-century
fortification enclosed an area slightly larger than the old Viking city.
The work was undertaken by the new Anglo-Norman inhabitants in
response to an order given around 1185 by Prince John to fortify the
city. With the exception of Reginald's Tower and the sections of wall
already described, nothing now remains above ground of these
sturdy, ancient defences.

FROM ST MARTIN'S GATE TO ST JOHN'S BRIDGE

During the mid-thirteenth century, in the reign of King Henry III, it
was decided to enclose the suburbs now springing up outside the old
Viking city. This work began at St Martin's Gate and a defensive wall
or possibly, in the early stages, an earthen bank and ditch, ran across
Parnell Street and down to St John's Bridge. Certainly by the late
Middle Ages a stone wall enclosed this area. As only small fragments
of this wall and what was a very substantial gate at St John's Bridge
remain, it is suggested that you walk to St John's Bridge via the
Applemarket and John's Street.

St John's Bridge, the oldest functioning urban bridge in Ireland,
was built sometime before 1199. It was in all probability built at the
instigation of King John, who is known to have had a great interest in
bridge-building. The bridge and gate marked the entry point of one
of the major roadways into the medieval city from Passage East. The
oldest section of the bridge is a very narrow structure, only wide
enough to allow a horse-drawn wagon to cross the river and enter the
city via St John's Gate. In 1368 this bridge was the scene of a battle
when the Powers and their allies, the O'Driscolls, long-time enemies
of the city, tried to gain access. Victory went to the mayor and his
army, though twenty-four of the better men of the city were slain.
The bridge was widened in 1765: observe the rounded eighteenth-
century arches on the downstream side, while on the upstream side
are slightly pointed twelfth-century arches.

FROM ST JOHN'S BRIDGE TO THE WATCH TOWER

Walking from the bridge to the Watch Tower, you pass the remains of a bastion tower. This tower would have projected out from the line of the city wall into the river, which in medieval times would have been much wider. The bastion was supported by a number of arches through which the river flowed; you can still detect the top of these arches at ground level in Mendicity Lane. A map dated 1590, on display at Waterford Museum of Treasures, shows that the bastion had cannon mounted on it to protect the bridge and St John's Gate from river-borne attack. Archaeological excavations carried out here by Waterford Corporation found that in about 1700 the tower had been used as a tanning vat – the owner of that leather-curing business was the great-grandfather of William Penrose, one of the founders of the Waterford Glass Factory in 1783.

THE WATCH TOWER

Its cylindrical shape suggests that this tower dates from the thirteenth century. However, you will observe that the openings are gun-loops and not arrow-loops, indicating that the tower was modified in

The Watch Tower, Railway Square.

the late fifteenth or early sixteenth century to accommodate artillery. At the rear of the tower are two entrances: one at ground level and a second at wall-walk level. The absence of windows on the inner elevation of the tower suggests that it functioned exclusively as a defensive structure and was not intended to be occupied as a residence during peacetime. Close Gate once stood where the main road runs today; it was demolished in the eighteenth century by Bullocks Wyse of the Manor of St John to provide easier access to his estate.

FROM THE WATCH TOWER TO THE DOUBLE TOWER

Before you cross over Manor Street to reach the Double Tower, take a look to the northeast and you will see the remains of the church belonging to the Benedictine priory of St John, founded in about 1190 and endowed by King John. The friary was a daughter house of the Benedictine priory in Bath, England. At the time of the dissolution of the monasteries by Henry VIII the friary passed to William Wyse, mayor of Waterford and a great friend of the king from whom he had already received the sword and cap of maintenance. As you proceed up Castle Street you will pass a stretch of wall with gun-loops or small cannon openings; the embrasures associated with these gun-loops can be seen clearly on the inner face of the wall. You can also see, on the inner face, the remains of the wall-walk that would have projected out from the top of the wall.

The Double Tower, Castle Street.

The Double Tower is so-called because it contains two chambers and in medieval times it would have provided access to the Benedictine church for the monks whose monastery and substantial lands and property lay outside the walls of the town. During the Cromwellian siege of the city in 1649, this tower and section of the town wall were pounded by cannon fire. These towers were not built with cannon in mind and therefore required bolstering – the Double Tower was half-filled with earth to help take the impact of the cannon fire. At this time also outer earthenworks were built both to take the impact of cannon and to inhibit access.

FROM THE DOUBLE TOWER TO THE FRENCH TOWER

Continuing up Castle Street the section of wall that projects outward is known as the ramparts. The ramparts belong to the age of gunpowder and may be interpreted as a platform for heavy guns. Fear of Spanish invasion during the 1580s and 1590s resulted in the upgrading of the city's defences, and it is thought that the ramparts date from this period. Others believe that they could have been constructed half a century later, coinciding with the period of the Catholic confederacy and the Cromwellian sieges. We know from Elizabethan maps, c.1590, that not only were the city's defences upgraded at this time but those of the harbour were also improved. The defences at Passage East, County Waterford, were also upgraded by the citizens to protect the harbour entrance, and on the opposite shore Duncannon Fort, in County Wexford, was built.

THE FRENCH TOWER

The top of Castle Street is dominated by the French Tower with its commanding view out over the surrounding countryside. The tower is

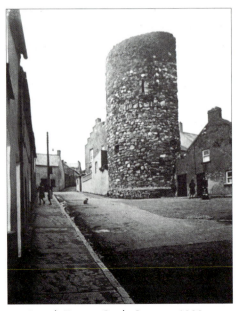

French Tower, Castle Street, c.1900.

kidney-shaped, which offers the maximum defensive view of the area outside the wall while occupying as little space as possible inside the wall. The ground and first floor of the tower date from the mid-thirteenth century when King Henry III allowed the corporation to collect taxes to finance the fortification of the suburbs. The upper floors were probably added in the fifteenth century to accommodate small guns and light cannon.

FROM THE FRENCH TOWER TO THE SEMI-LUNAR TOWER

As you follow the town wall along Browne's Lane you will see, roughly midway along this section, the remains of a tower that afforded protection to this length of the wall. The wall terminated at the New Gate, which was not built until the second half of the fifteenth century. Though the gate has long since vanished, its memory is still preserved in the street name: Newgate Street.

Opposite the site of New Gate a wall plaque denotes the site of St Stephen's Leper Hospital, founded by King John during one of his visits to Waterford. It appears that John, having partaken of too much cider, wine and fresh Irish salmon while in Waterford, became severely ill and feared that he had contracted leprosy, a disease brought back from the Crusades. He promised the Almighty that he would build a leper hospital if he were spared. John survived, and true to his word a leper hospital was built at Waterford dedicated to St Stephen. John endowed the hospital with a large tract of land, the rents of which maintained the institution. The land is situated between the city and the beautiful seaside fishing village of Dunmore East, and to this day the area is known as Leperstown.

All that remains of the hospital today is the house of the hospital master, rebuilt in 1637 on the same site, though its name is remembered in Stephen Street, which was laid out in the early thirteenth century to give access to both the hospital and the church attached to it. A statue of St Stephen, the first Christian martyr, on display at Waterford Museum of Treasures, was very probably rescued from the hospital during the Reformation. This simple wooden statue shows the saint holding a stone, the symbol of his martyrdom; he was stoned to death.

A new leper hospital, also dedicated to St Stephen and designed by John Roberts, was built on John's Hill in 1785, though by that stage leprosy had almost disappeared from Ireland. In 1896 the hospital was renamed the County and City Infirmary. This hospital closed in 1986, though the charity fund of the Hospital of St Stephen continues to exist and its master, like that of the Holy Ghost Hospital, is still held in high esteem in the city. Today revenue from the charity's endowment, which dates back to King John in the early thirteenth century, is used to purchase hi-tech medical equipment for Waterford Regional Hospital.

The Semi-Lunar Tower at the rear of St Stephen's National School.

As you walk into Stephen Street, you will find the town wall continues to the rear of the houses on your left, you can reach it by walking through an opening in the row of houses. The large, old, red sandstone house close to the town wall dates to c.1690 and is said to have been built as a home for sailors. The wall is truncated by Bachelor's Walk, however when you cross this street you will see on the truncated cross-section of town wall a green plaque showing the location of the Semi-Lunar Tower.

To gain access to the Semi-Lunar or Half Moon Tower, walk to the top of Bachelor's Walk, turn right into Mayor's Walk and at the end of that street turn right again to go down Patrick Street. On the left at the top of Patrick Street you will see a blue plaque marking the site of St Patrick's Gate, which was demolished during the eighteenth century. On your right you will notice the point at which the city wall met St Patrick's Gate; it is covered by an iron railing. The large building that stands on the top of Patrick Street is the monastery of the De La Salle brothers. If you walk around to the rear of the monastery a key to the garden, where the Semi-Lunar Tower stands, can be obtained. Please note that the monastery grounds are private property, so access to the garden is available only during reasonable hours and at the discretion of the owners.

SEMI-LUNAR TOWER

Like the Double Tower in Castle Street, the Semi-Lunar Tower is a flanking or on-the-wall tower. The purpose of these towers was to make defending the wall easier because attackers who attempted to scale the wall could be repulsed by archers from the relative safety of the protruding tower. Because the tower rose well above the wall level it could be used to defend the adjacent wall-walk and act as a lookout and signalling post. The tower is vaulted at both the first level and at battlement level, with no connecting stairs. The fact that there is no connecting stairs suggests that the lower half of the monument was, like most of the other towers on the circuit, built in the thirteenth century, and like the others it too was substantially altered towards the end of the Middle Ages to accommodate artillery.

FROM THE SEMI-LUNAR TOWER TO THE BEACH TOWER

Once you have viewed the Semi-Lunar Tower return to Patrick Street, turn right and proceed downhill for about fifty metres. To the left you will see the entrance to Carrigeen Park. The name is derived from the Irish and means Little Rock. During the Middle Ages the area was known as Cow Rock because a cattlemart was held here. Proceed along Carrigeen Park until you come to the upper level of the Beach Tower. This tower, with its fifteenth-century crenellations, is one of the finest on the circuit. It was built on a rocky outcrop that forms a natural defensive position. During the medieval period the area between the tower and the river was not developed so the tower would have commanded a fine view of the river. From the upper battlements you can see Granagh Castle, located upriver on the banks of the Suir.

From the Beach Tower proceed to King's Terrace with its tall eighteenth-century houses. Before heading down the steps, note the blue plaque on the wall to your left. This wall is part of St Patrick's Fort, built originally of earth and timber during Queen Elizabeth's reign, c.1590. As in the case of other extensions to the medieval defences, fear of a Spanish invasion was the reason for its construction. The fort was substantially rebuilt during the early seventeenth century as a bastion citadel. Built outside the town wall it has a rectangular plan with corner bastions typical of many seventeenth-century forts in Ireland.

Proceed down the Stony Steps and turn right. Continue right to the lower level of the Beach Tower, together with the town wall now running north to the river, will come into view. This is the last visible section of the wall though portions of it are incorporated into buildings between here and the river. As this section of the wall approached the river, it turned

The Beach Tower at Jenkin's Lane.

right to form the quayside defences of the Anglo-Norman extension. This wall ran parallel to the river and joined the old Viking triangular city at Turgesius's Tower. The tower was located roughly some metres from where the present-day Clock Tower stands, at the intersection of Barronstrand Street and the quay. At this point the wall continued up the quay to Reginald's Tower and south to St Martin's Gate. These stretches of wall and the towers and gates along them, now defunct, were demolished in the early eighteenth century. Interestingly, excavations along the line of the wall reveal that even where it has been removed its influence has not been lost, because the new merchants' houses built along the quay in the eighteenth century used the base of the wall as a foundation for their houses.

Granagh Castle, on the banks of the River Suir, near Waterford.

WILLIAM VINCENT WALLACE PLAZA

William Vincent Wallace Plaza and Marina.

Waterford Corporation's stunning new plaza was built as the city's millennium project in 2000 and officially opened in 2001. It functions as an amenity area where the goings and comings of the river can be savoured and performances can be enjoyed. A continuous walkway along the edge of the river connects the plaza to Rice Bridge and provides a most pleasant walk, particularly on a summer's even-

ing. The plaza is dedicated to William Vincent Wallace (1812–1865). Wallace, born in Colbeck Street, was one of Waterford's most colourful sons, famous for his operas *Maritana*, *Lurline* and *Amber Witch*. He is regarded as one of the greatest nineteenth-century composers of English opera. He was married three times and lived the life of an adventurer, travelling the world extensively, sometimes giving concerts in out of the way places and accepting sheep and poultry as payment in kind. He went whale-fishing in Australia, crossed the Andes by

Rotating sculpture in the new plaza.

mule and gave concerts in Jamaica. Wallace performed as a violinist in New York, Philadelphia, Baltimore and New Orleans, and was a founder member of the New York Philharmonic Society. He died in France in 1865, aged fifty-three.

THE PEOPLE'S PARK

The People's Park is about a ten minute walk from the city centre. It was laid out in 1857 and has both formal and informal areas and a children's play area. The park is connected by an iron bridge to the city courthouse, which

The bandstand in People's Park.

was built on the site of the medieval St Catherine's Abbey. Opened in 1849, it was one of the achievements of the reformed corporation that administered the city from 1841 onwards.

SPORT AND LEISURE

When God created Waterford, He must have had golfers in mind. Not only are the courses themselves both spectacular and challenging but the stunning scenery which surrounds them is positively breath-taking. The Waterford Municipal Golf Course, set on 130 acres of rolling countryside at Williamstown, Waterford, is one of the best in the country. Designed by top course architect Eddie Hackett, it is one of the longest inland 18-hole courses in Ireland. Existing land features are used to maximum effect to create a beautiful and challenging environment for golfers. Other renowned courses can be found at Waterford Castle and close to the city at Dunmore East, Faithlegg, Tramore and Dungarvan. (For a full listing of Waterford's golf courses contact the Tourist Office.)

The Regional Sports Centre, built by Waterford Corporation, is located in the suburbs with entrances from both the Tramore and Cork roads. The centre boasts fine gym facilities, pitch and putt, tennis courts, indoor basketball, football, all-weather running track and a stadium and stand with seating facilities. Also on the Cork Road is the Waterford Crystal Sports Complex, comprising playing pitches, gym and an indoor heated swimming pool that is open to the public.

THE RIVER SUIR

The ancient Irish annals, *An Leabhar Gabhála*, the Book of Conquests, has this to say about Waterford harbour:

> A sweet confluence of waters, a trinity of rivers,
> Was their first resting place,
> They unloaded the women and the sensual idol.

This refers to the three rivers that meet the sea in Waterford Harbour: the Barrow, Nore and Suir. Traditionally, these are collectively known as the Three Sisters because the word *suir* derives from the Irish word *tSiúir*, which literally means 'the sister'. Between them, these three great rivers drain a quarter of the landmass of Ireland.

ineteenth-century photograph of Timbertoes, the first bridge built over the River Suir (1793).

In its long journey to the sea from where it rises at the Devil's Bit Mountain in County Tipperary, the River Suir wanders through some of the finest land in Ireland. Waterford, as the main port to satisfy the needs of this wealthy hinterland, grew rich on river-borne trade. In his famous work *The Faerie Queene*, the Elizabethan poet Edmund Spenser turns away from the contemplation of fictitious landscapes to praise the rivers of Ireland:

> The gentle Shure, that making way,
> by sweet Clonmel, adorns rich Waterford.
> All which long sundered do at last accord,
> To join in one ere to the sea they come,
> So flowing all for one, all one at last become.

It is interesting to note Spenser's rendering of the correct Irish pronunciation of the word *suir*, which he must surely have learned from the lips of the locals.

Waterford harbour has acted as an entry point to the southeast of Ireland since time immemorial. Long before Norse times, seafarers crossed St George's Channel from Wales to Waterford, and conversely, men of the Decies, a Gaelic tribe from County Waterford, sailed out from here and settled in southwestern Wales, bringing with them the tradition of erecting Ogham stones to mark the burials of important members of their clan. Pre-Patrician missionaries came to Ireland by this route and even in Norman times it was still the preferred route into Ireland, with the crossing from the Bristol Channel a shorter and more hospitable one than that through the wild and inhospitable reaches of north Wales.

The journey upriver from Hook Head and Dunmore East is among the most scenic in Ireland. The incoming traveller passes headland and inlet, goes under the battlements of Duncannon Fort and past Passage East – one of the most ancient and historic ferry-crossings in Ireland – to enter the magnificent reach of river beyond Ballyhack to Nook and Buttermilk Point, which looks like a dramatic Norwegian fjord, and then to the Meeting of the Waters at Cheekpoint (Fairy Point in Irish).

The magical spot where the combined waters of the Barrow and the Nore meet the lordly Suir is nothing less than a journey through history. Invaders, kings, princes, merchants have all landed here. Emigrants have departed from here to places around the globe. Castles, abbeys, age-old fishing weirs, great houses, comfortable farms, simple boat landings and commerce crowd in upon the waterway.

All through the ages, it has been the river at Waterford and the views of Waterford from or across the River Suir which have most impressed travellers. Raymond Piper best summed it up: 'The Suir is a wide river, as wide as the Thames at Westminster Bridge, three times as wide as the Seine or Tiber, five times the width of the Liffey at O'Connell Bridge. It is this width of stream, which gives the city its open airy look, a handsome well situated city.'

Today as people arrive by pleasure boat, by great liner or by merchant ship at this most ancient of Irish cities, it is the long, composed and harmonious look of the quay at Waterford that reflects the history and commerce of Vadrarfjord, Port Láirge, Waterford: the pleasantest of Irish cities.

Historic Waterford provides a spectacular backdrop to the modern plaza and marina
– the new face of Waterford city.

OTHER BOOKS IN THE
O'BRIEN PRESS
CITY GUIDES SERIES

DISCOVER DERRY
Brian Lacey

This book tells the fascinating story of Derry, in words and pictures, from the sixth century to the present day. Part one explores the history of Derry through key events, including the founding of the Early Christian Church, the first English invasion in 1566, the Apprentice Boys' rebellion and the Troubles of the twentieth century. Part two visits Derry's most interesting buildings and landmarks, including: the city walls, the Guildhall, the Memorial Hall, St Columb's Cathedral, Magee College and the Quayside.

Paperback £9.99/€12.68/$16.95

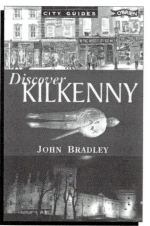

DISCOVER KILKENNY
John Bradley

Kilkenny has long been noted as Ireland's foremost medieval town. This is the story of its long and fascinating history. Part one explores the history of Kilkenny through key events, including the founding of the Early Christian monastery, the coming of the Normans and the witchcraft trial of Alice Kyteler. Part two visits Kilkenny's most interesting buildings and landmarks, including Kilkenny Castle, St Canice's Cathedral and Rothe House.

Paperback £9.99/€12.68/$16.95

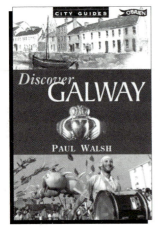

DISCOVER GALWAY
Paul Walsh

Galway is a vibrant, exuberant place with a tangible charm. This book presents the history of this unique city. Part one explores the history of the city, which spans almost ten centuries, including the lives of the townspeople, the architecture of the buildings, religion and politics and development in modern times. Part two provides a guide to the historic places and buildings, including St Nicholas's Church, Lynch's and Blake's Castles, the Cathedral, Eyre Square, the Spanish Arch and Fish Market and the Claddagh.

Paperback £9.99/€12.68/$16.95

Send for our full-colour catalogue

ORDER FORM

Please send me the books as marked.

I enclose cheque/postal order for £ . . . . (+£1.00 P&P per title)
OR please charge my credit card ☐ Access/Mastercard ☐ Visa

Card Number __ __ __ __   __ __ __ __   __ __ __ __   __ __ __ __

Expiry Date __ __/__ __

Name. . . . . Tel . . . .

Address . . . .

. . . .

Please send orders to: THE O'BRIEN PRESS, 20 Victoria Road, Dublin 6.
Tel: +353 1 4923333; Fax: + 353 1 4922777; E-mail: books@obrien.ie
Website: www.obrien.ie
Note: prices subject to change without notice